# Men Are a Luxury, Not a Necessity

## Nena Burnette, LPC, Vonda Boston Keasler, LMFT

BALBOA.
PRESS
A DIVISION OF HAY HOUSE

Balboa Press books may be ordered through booksellers or by contacting:

Balboa Press
A Division of Hay House
1663 Liberty Drive
Bloomington, IN 47403
www.balboapress.com
1 (877) 407-4847

Because of the dynamic nature of the Internet, any web addresses or links contained in this book may have changed since publication and may no longer be valid. The views expressed in this work are solely those of the authors and do not necessarily reflect the views of the publisher, and the publisher hereby disclaims any responsibility for them.

The authors of this book does not dispense medical advice or prescribe the use of any technique as a form of treatment for physical, emotional, or medical problems without the advice of a physician, either directly or indirectly. The intent of the authors is only to offer information of a general nature to help you in your quest for emotional and spiritual well-being. In the event you use any of the information in this book for yourself, which is your constitutional right, the authors and the publisher assume no responsibility for your actions.

Any people depicted in stock imagery provided by Getty Images are models, and such images are being used for illustrative purposes only.
Certain stock imagery © Getty Images.

Print information available on the last page.

ISBN: 978-1-9822-0414-3 (sc)
ISBN: 978-1-9822-0416-7 (hc)
ISBN: 978-1-9822-0415-0 (e)

Library of Congress Control Number: 2018905659

Balboa Press rev. date:    05/17/2018

# Table of Contents

# Nena's Introduction

This book has been rumbling around in my head for about thirty years. I have started and restarted many times. It has been a difficult undertaking. It feels a bit like standing in the middle of town naked, but I feel the need for this book is out there. So, try not to picture me naked.

About a year ago, I enlisted the help of my friend and colleague as a partner in getting this project done. She is a licensed marriage and family therapist and also clergy. My purpose for this book is that I have through my various careers come to have much too much information as is comfortable at times about dysfunction in families. Families begin with a couple, and I have seen poorly matched couples create havoc and mayhem within their families that ultimately gets perpetuated over and over.

While I want this book to be utilized by therapists, I also want the general public to seek it out too and relate to the book. Thus, we have intentionally written it at a high school level with non-diagnostic, therapy terminology. It is also important for me in this publication and in my life, in general, to have some laughs along the way. Fair warning: there will also be tears.

Every day I see families, and individuals who, had they been emotionally healthier and shopped more efficiently for mates, would most likely not be in the situations that lead them to my office. In addition, if the parents were dysfunctional, the children show up at my door more often than not as adults trying to cope. I have seen and continue to see the generations of cycles of abuse and of unhappiness that perpetuates itself over and over. I know this to be true because, having worked in similar fields for thirty some odd years, I have seen generations of the same families make the same mistakes over and over, more often than not, passing into the next generations with no end in sight. I am currently a mental health therapist, but I have also done child welfare and nursing. I've seen the same in each of these fields; often times I have seen one family across all three fields. I see children of children of children...you get the picture...make the same poor choices over and over making another generation near inevitable. I am not saying that poor self-worth and self-knowledge combined with poor definition of relationships are the only culprits, but they are definitely in the top two.

The idea of this book has been there about thirty years, but the idea, the understanding, has been back there as far as I can remember. I saw the demise of my mother's first marriage. I caught just a glimpse into how dysfunctional and damaging it was. Even at my young age, I knew there had to be something better.

Then my Mom found my Dad. It was and is still beautiful. They are in their 80's and 90's and still are deeply in love, having fun together, and they remain the tightly woven helm of our family. They are still traveling both together and with all of us in big groups. I have had good role models, and I am very thankful for my parents.

I made up my mind during my teenage years to find what they have. I had to experiment like everyone else to find what traits and communication styles fit me best, and of course, someone to have fun with while still having that steadfast, safe, real luxury. *REAL* knowledge in my gut that this was my luxury.

I was lucky and blessed enough to have a healthy, eccentric family that taught me to love life and always made sure I knew I belonged and was as precious to all of them as they were and are to me.

I did have some issues as all do, but underneath, I knew in my soul that those issues were already worked out. No lasting trauma. Everlasting love and support. I had a healthy base to look for my luxury.

Few find their luxury in their teens, but I did. I knew what I wanted, and I knew that he was it. We were set up, and I knew almost immediately that this 'redneck' was for me. Somehow, I knew that he would stick by me. Grow with me. Hold me up and be my life partner.

Some years ago, a naïve teen ager asked me why I would marry a redneck. My response was, "oh I don't know, he worked his ass off to support his family, he grew with me and held down the fort through three degrees, he is a wonderful father, and he worships the ground I walk on. That a good enough reason?" She was speechless.

Though this book is meant to be educational and outline a psychological paradigm shift as to how we look for and choose a mate, we both share parts of our personal, and until now, private feelings and information, the reason being that all that we have seen and worked with as therapists is confidential, and we hesitate to put anything in that someone might read and say "damn, that's me." In addition, I know my story better than anyone else's. Also, I have always looked at and learned the base of the thought process through my own eyes and experiences.

There is solid theory behind the aforementioned paradigm shift that I will share. However, I want this to read as a thoughtful, educational book but also with real life and humor. Let's face it; we have to have a sense of humor to engage in any relationship and in life. Sometimes you just have to shake your head and laugh.

My goal for you in the book is to think over the proposed paradigm shift, learn whether or not you have positive self-worth, self-esteem, and learn how to be emotionally healthy. It is from this base that you learn whether or not you can visualize what your luxury will be. Learn how to treat, communicate with, and appreciate your luxury on all levels. Also, it is important to me that you have a laugh, even if it is at my expense.

# Vonda's Introduction

Several years ago, my dear friend, Nena, asked me to read part of a book she was writing with the catchy title *Men are a Luxury, Not a Necessity*. She wanted my input as to whether or not I thought I was a worthwhile pursuit. I loved what she had written and encouraged her to complete it. In the work that we do over and over again, we see generational dysfunction, relationships that just happen and the result often being, children who just happen, and thus repeats more the same poor or self-destructive choices.

I was honored when she asked me several months ago to join her in bringing this book to fruition. It has been an amazing partnership in which we have played off each other's ideas and suggestions. Throughout the course of writing and sometimes just talking about writing, we have shared each other's own personal stories. We have grown in our partnership, friendship, and have touched each other's lives in ways too numerous to even share. We have each shared personal experience in this book in hoping that each of our readers might reflect on their own life experiences as they journey toward self-enlightenment, journey to their luxury, or with their luxury. Once again, thank you, My Friend, for inviting me on this journey. Friends are a necessity, and a luxury.

# History of Marriage

There are many things that Nena and I have in common. Many core principles that we share have allowed us to develop a friendship, first as colleagues with the Human Services sector of the State of Arkansas, then as working mothers married to Arkansas born and bred men who worked hard for a living and supported their out spoken, compassionate wives as they returned to school to get social work Bachelor's degrees, and Master's degrees in Rehab Counseling and Marriage and Family Therapy.

Among our differences, Nena grew up in Arkansas, part of a close, blended family. Her parents were both professionals, a public-school educator turned long-term administrator of a local factory in Paragould and a retired nurse.

I grew up in rural Michigan, my parents, laborers in local factories, later my father a local union steward, promoted to union president. Then he was a union laborer in asphalt construction. Later, my mother worked in the health care sector as an aid and then private music teacher and a college music student. She had the capacity as an eighteen-year-old young woman to have a career as a professional musician, a three-octave soprano. She chose marriage and children instead. In the 1950's, women could not have it all.

The men in my family on both sides worked hard in demanding, physical blue-collar jobs. I come from a long line of carpenters, machinists, and auto industry workers. Throw in some lumber jacks and road builders and your mind's eye sees dirty, hardworking men who could fix anything, who unionized, who were part of what we call the rust that built America.

The women in my family worked hard, often times in health care or hospitality. They changed beds, cleaned bathrooms, and cared for the elderly and sick of their families or of the community. I come from a long line of maids, nurse's aides and bar workers. My mother, her mother, and her sisters all worked in the local state facility for the mentally retarded. One of my first jobs was a weekend house parent to the group home for the mentally retarded adult men three blocks from my home.

I was born in the middle of the 20th century. Many things were worse at the start of the 20th century than they are today. In the early 1900's, thousands of children worked full time in mines, mills, and sweatshops. Most workers labored ten hours a day, most often six days per week, which left them little time or energy for family life. Race riots were more frequent and often deadlier that those experienced by recent generations, although we certainly have seen race riots in our lifetimes.

Wage riots and union organization saw their beginnings as workers began to find ways of gaining a voice. Women couldn't vote, and their wages were so low that prostitution was sometimes the only way a woman could support herself and her children. In 1900, a white child had one chance in three of losing a brother or sister before age fifteen, and a Black child had a 50-50 chance of seeing a sibling die. Children's aid groups reported widespread abuse and neglect by parents. Men who deserted or divorced their wives rarely paid child support. Only six percent of the children graduated high school, compared with eighty two percent today.

Much nostalgia for the 1950's is a result of selective amnesia- the same process that makes childhood memories of summer vacations grow sunnier with each passing year. The superficial sameness of 1950's family life was achieved through censorship, coercion and discrimination. People with unconventional beliefs faced governmental investigation and arbitrary firings. African Americans and Mexican Americans were prevented from voting in some states by literacy tests that were not administered to whites. Individuals who didn't follow the rigid gender and sexual rules of the day were ostracized.

*Leave It to Beaver* did not reflect the real-life experience of most American families. While many moved into the middle class during the 1950's, poverty remained more widespread than in the worst of our last three recessions. More children went hungry, and poverty rates for the elderly were more than twice as high as today. A number of historical factors contributed to shifts in how Americans perceived and participate in family structure. According to the American Bar Association, in 1965, the Supreme Court extended constitutional protections for "various forms of reproductive freedom" through its ruling in Griswold v. Connecticut. There were also medical advances in contraception, including the invention of the birth control pill in 1960. As a result, the way children were brought into families became more varied than ever. Divorce changed during the 1960's as well. In 1969, California became "the first state to adopt a no-fault divorce, permitting parties to end their marriage simply upon showing irreconcilable differences" and within sixteen years, every other state had followed suit.

In 2017, the divorce rate for first marriages—meaning a marriage in which neither person has been married before – is reportedly between 40 and 50 %. But for second marriages, in which at least one of the spouses has been married once before, the rate jumps to between 60 and 67%. The more time someone has been married the greater the chance of divorce becomes.

# Men are a Luxury, Not a Necessity

My husband and I have been married thirty-three years. I won't say that it has been all roses and fairy tales, but I wouldn't trade a minute of it. On the surface, we appear to be a weird cross between Dan and Roseanne Connor and Jill and Tim Taylor! Weird thought huh? If you really take that in, you realize that we appear to be a strange couple. However, upon a modest examination, you immediately see a very strong, close relationship. We are each other's luxury in life. We enjoy and crave each other's company. We stabilize each other.

He and I are soul mates. However, if you think we are alike, mirror images of each other, you couldn't be further from the truth. We are kindred spirits, each leaning on the other, interconnected but completely different, even opposite, in so many ways. Our souls are connected but not duplicates of the other. How, do you say?

I shopped differently than many people do. I did not need a man. I desired a companion, a partner…a luxury to make my life more comfortable and to have someone with which to share the ride, the dash between birth and death. And he has completely been my partner, my confidant, my best friend, and my lover. When I wanted to change my career and chase dreams, even though they were not his dreams…He came along for the long and bumpy ride, willingly and without hesitation. He believed in me without question or doubt. Through each stage of our life, we identified goals and planned, knowing that life never goes according to plan. We accepted this because we knew whatever curve was thrown at us, we would be together and we would work it into our lives.

We have faced many obstacles. We lost his younger fifteen-year-old brother eleven days before our son was born. It was an unimaginable tragedy followed immediately by the miracle of child birth. Our son came into the world looking just like his uncle Steven. It was ecstatic and heart breaking at the same time.

Some years later, when I was on a good roll of writing this book, my sister Sally was diagnosed with cancer and died in less than four months. Shortly after, a brother diagnosed, then another sister, then a brother died of complications of open heart surgery. Next, my sister died and, finally, nine years after my first sister, my last brother died.

Needless to say, somewhere in there I stopped writing for a long intermission. My luxury, however, never faltered a step in maintaining his role in my life. He held me while I cried. He cried while I screamed. He picked me up when I fell down. He took all the household and adult child related responsibilities over all alone. He protected me from outside life so that I could be with my family, take care of them. He took care of me in every possible way. When the nightmares started, he trained himself to sleep with one hand on me at all times.

During all this, we launched two children into the world on their own. We watched with pride as one married and later made us grandparents. The other followed academia straight through gaining a Master's Degree in English. Since then, she has found her luxury, and we couldn't be happier. We have been through sickness, childbirth and child rearing, extended family catastrophes and celebrations, and finally empty nest. Unlike some couples, empty nest is not a trauma for us; it is merely another exciting part of the adventure, time to be just us again, and that is an exciting thing. These past thirty-three years have been an adventure of mammoth proportions, both beautiful beyond words and tragic beyond words. I could have faced all this without him, but I am thankful to God each day that I have my husband to share the adventure.

This man is not just someone I picked up off the streets, at a bar, Walmart, or even a dating site. This man was chosen well for all the above-mentioned strengths, love for me, and other reasons I still cannot put into words. A few songs come to mind: "Young Love" by the Judd's, "Wild Angels" by Martina McBride, "Remember When" by Alan Jackson and finally Jimmy Buffett's "Nothing but a Breeze." We are in the midst of an amazing adventure that has had its ups and downs, but always looking toward the future together, just my luxury and me.

I have always told my daughter, "Men are a Luxury, Not a Necessity." Please understand, this is not a man-bashing statement. It is, instead, an analogy, an epiphany, a paradigm shift, to try to change the way women view couple hood, thus changing the way they shop for a partner. As a therapist, I know that at least once each week, I say the words, "Honey, you're fishing in the wrong pond."

Women often tie their value as a human being into being part of a couple, possibly even more so in the south. We are cultured and nursed toward this from birth throughout life. Both our families, and our environment entrench this thought, this fiercely limiting internal belief into our very soul. Who among us does not remember granny constantly grieving the "fact" that the beautiful, young Ellie Mae was an old maid? Even while watching these episodes, we laughed. But still, it was assimilated into our minds and filed solidly amid the matter of our brain.

Again, how many remember the reason young female high school graduates were first sent to college? Not for the education, certainly, but instead to get an "MRS" degree. And along with that, parents of young males entering college were encouraged to use this venue as a shopping center for a mate, a mate whose sole purpose would be to support their career and give them promising children, not to achieve her own college degree and develop a career or even a separate identity. Once the "MRS" degree was obtained, the young lady's job then became to mold herself into whatever best suited her husband and her career

Speaking again of shopping, this is certainly not only a good analogy, but is in fact, what we do. We shop for the person we want to spend our lives with. Or, at least, we *should* shop. Many do not. Please take into consideration, though, there are different kinds of shopping, each with different goals and sets of rules to define the shopping experience and outcome.

Take, for instance, the chore of shopping for basic necessities. A necessity is something we have to have to support life: food, shelter, water, etcetera. When we shop for a necessity, the methodology of the experience is very narrowly defined. We have to have it to go on with our lives. So, we look for the quickest, most economical selection. And let's face it, we usually do so in a hurry and do not put a lot of analysis into what we buy. We do very little, if any, comparison shopping. We have to have food; therefore, we run through a grocery store grabbing up sale items, quick fixes to keep us alive while we move toward the real goals of our fast-paced hectic lives. It is just the way it is.

This is truly how many, if not most, women (and arguably men) shop for a mate. They feel they have to be married or in a relationship to be whole, to be taken care of or to be valued in society. So, if you think about the way this is achieved, it is very much like a mad dash through Walmart to pick up feminine products before that time hits. And while you may have a preference of that product, your brain says that time is running out. Let's face it ladies, you are going to take what is on the shelf and hope for the best…not a good idea for feminine products, and most definitely not a good idea for shopping for a mate for LIFE.

A *luxury*, though, is an entirely different animal. A luxury is something that we can live without; not having it does not determine whether or not we survive until tomorrow. It is something completely nonessential to our lives that we desire because of what it does for us, for its quality, and for how it enriches our lives.

We have to have certain preset factors (or milestones) present to obtain, or for that matter, even to desire a luxury. Our basic needs have to be met, or we are unable to even conceive of the idea of a luxury. It is really hard to conceive of a Disney vacation and how this can enrich your life when there are no groceries in the house on the 15th, and you have no way of obtaining more until the 1st. A vacation does not even enter your unconscious, much less, your conscious thoughts.

This is a time, however, when women shop quickly for a mate. I recently was told that a woman I know let her husband come back home after beating her up. Her reason…she stated matter of factly…" the utilities were shut off, and I didn't have the money, and he said he would pay the electric and water bill if I would take him back." She also added, "I've been beaten way worse than he did anyway."

When approached by the fact that he did not acknowledge any wrong or even promise not to do it again, she again responded, "it's not a big deal; it wasn't that bad of a beating." This is the state of many relationships that I encounter every day. I am sure that you do as well. The answer? A paradigm shift. Teach women, and men as well, maybe *especially* children, how to shop for a mate making an informed decision, versus decision by default.

To understand a luxury, there are prerequisites that must be met. We have to have had either a fairly chaos or abuse-free childhood. Those who did not have to play catch up and learn all the things that the lucky ones with nurturing childhoods learned growing up. Those who were unlucky in childhood have to search and learn to develop all the milestones from basic needs to nearing self-actualization, or at least be on the path. This is indeed an intimidating adventure. This is where we, as counselors, mentors, neighbors, teachers, grandparents, and even the community comes in. We have to give, teach, and lift up these who are not ready to shop for a luxury and give support, guidance, and love along the way as they take their first part of the journey of the dash alone with support systems in place. People, and even pets, that give unconditional love teach what belongingness feels like. What self-worth feels like. How to navigate life alone with friends and family to love, support, and guide them, just as we teach them to cook, put gas in the car, and pay bills. So, must we teach them, initially about being a healthy individual, then about couple hood at its best. A luxury instead of a necessity.

When we have made that journey to healthy individual, and begin to feel we are ready, we deserve and we have earned the privilege of a luxury…the search begins. We have to feel safe and have a certain sense of belonging in our family, community, and society as a whole. We have to be comfortable in our own circumstances. We have to be confident we can utilize, fuel and maintain a luxury.

What constitutes a luxury means different things to different people according to their personality, lifestyles, and values. To determine what this means to us, we have to know ourselves intrinsically, our soul, what makes who we are deep inside. When you know that, you can then define what will compliment that package that is our heart, soul, our life.

For me, that feeling comes from sitting by, in, or on the ocean, hearing the waves break, feeling and smelling the sea air, palm trees swaying, or dolphins frolicking alongside a cruise ship. For me, for my soul, this is total and utter peace, made better only if my husband and or my family is with me. There is a tiny open bar on the edge of the water in Cozumel, Mexico that is my favorite place in the world. Immediate peace permeates every pore of my body, every inch of my soul. The second I sit down there and look out to the ocean, which is a luxury. And working your way toward such an enveloping luxury should, in itself, be an exciting and rewarding adventure.

Our adventurous travel toward our luxury should be stable, grounded with eyes wide open. It should simultaneously be electric with giddy angst. You should be at ease with this person without having to talk yourself into believing he is ok. He should demonstrate that he is safe, excited about you and who you are easily and openly. This should be both a learning adventure and a grand, exciting adventure. There should be fluidity, communication, and naturally occurring acceptance of each other that leads further and further toward becoming loosely but richly intertwined.

The first time I ever heard the name of my daughter's luxury, they weren't dating yet, but things were kindling. All she said was "Mom, he calls me pretty girl." It was a simple but loud statement. These few years later, they are a beautiful couple. I think it has been a grand adventurous trip and continues to be enrooted.

When one has embarked on the adventure for a luxury, the travel should be patient, open-eyed and stable. Enjoy the ride. Then when the travel is done, immerse yourself completely within the experience that the luxury provides. We do not, however, lose track of ourselves, our soul, who we are intrinsically. Just as I do not lose track of my family or my other responsibilities back at home while I'm sitting in that tiny ocean bar, I still am wrapped in the arms of luxury, something that soothes and feeds my soul.

Just as when I am with my husband, in peace and in crisis, I am wrapped in the arms of luxury. Never fails. He always comes through. I know, without a doubt, we will weather the storms; then we will sit on the beach or our porch hand-in-hand, and the feeling will be luxuriously peaceful. Neither do I lose track of who I am as an individual when dealing with daily life, no matter how stressful. I am who God meant me to be wherever I am; a luxury does not change that. However, if one does not have a necessity, it probably changes some aspect of who he or she is, or how one develops, and it alters the ability to envision and work toward a luxury.

So, to review, this luxury does not change who or what you are. It does, however, showcase or enhance the strengths and positive aspects of which you are, much like a good bra supports the girls…it does not change them. It just makes the picture a little higher quality

13

and offers support for an aching back. But, bra on or off, they are still the same girls.

When you decide you are ready for a luxury item in your life, you do not run haphazardly through a grocery store grabbing up items hoping that something will be the right choice to make a gourmet meal and enrich your night. No, of course not.

Instead, you spend time and energy defining just what you want from this luxury. You identify and even fantasize about just how it will fit into your life, making it more satisfying, how it will support and soothe away stress after a long, bad day. How its very presence will lend hope and optimism to your morning upon awakening. How your interaction with this luxury will feed your confidence so that you will obtain your goals. How this luxury will lend support while you develop the energy, the drive, and most of all, the support to fulfill your life's ambition and purpose. That luxury makes your life more enriched and satisfying. It does not determine whether or not your life exists and what your human identify or worth is.

Oh yes, to shop for this kind of luxury item takes extensive planning and goal setting. You have to define every nuance and quality of the type of luxury you want to support your lifestyle and choices. You desire a luxury that fits perfectly with who you are, and who you aspire to be. A luxury of this caliber also needs to be versatile in case who you want to be undergoes transformation so that it will adapt, support, and transform itself so that it will continue to fit perfectly within your life

You, in turn, must do the same for your luxury. You must define all the parameters of a luxury of this proportion before you even begin to shop. A frantic run through Walmart will not produce this valuable type of luxury item. Neither will one long, aisle-rambling trip through Walmart. This is the ultimate item that you are looking for. This is a marathon, not a sprint. This luxury item has a no-return policy, and if you shop and make your selection well, you certainly will never regret the no-return policy.

In that same vein, waking in the morning next to my husband, we wake slowly together and snuggle under the cover. We discuss the day, laugh, and joke together. We reminisce, we plan, and we hold each other. Sometimes the talk is serious; sometimes no sense at all comes from the conversation. But either way, it is always the most luxurious part of the day for me. It gives me the hope, initiative, and gentle reminder that even though the day may go smoothly or fall to crap within thirty minutes of leaving the driveway, by the end of the day, I will be back with him to share my feelings, my wins and defeats of the day. This knowledge makes what ever happened during the day easier to adjust to and deal with, an exciting challenge to face.

The first time I remember uttering the phrase that men are a luxury not a necessity was when my daughter was just a young child. At that time, it was only a thought, a desire for my daughter to grow up believing this and thus shopping well for a mate at the appropriate time for her. The appropriate time and person came for her during my absence from this endeavor, and I am very happy for them. Though not married, they are a happy couple. They have similar interests, they respect each other, and they are totally comfortable with each other as well as exorbitantly affectionate. In fact, one thing that my children have always laughed at my husband and I about is the practice he has of putting me to bed. I normally go to bed earlier than him, and he comes in and tucks me in and kisses me and tells me how much he loves me. This has been our practice through our whole marriage and our children have always laughed at it. Recently, my daughter shared with me that when she stays with her luxury and goes to bed early, he tucks her in. He has also been known to drive all the way out to her house to tuck her in and lock the door on his way out. Luxury.

Early on, I was doing the house wife thing. Yes. I have nothing but respect for those women and men who choose to stay at home with children. It does wonders for the children moving up through the stages toward self-actualization. If mom or dad are happy with decision and no one is being coerced into the role, it creates a very happy, healthy dynamic.

As time passed by, my children became more independent. I returned to the work force, back to nursing. I worked as an office nurse for a very small family practice clinic for a fabulous doctor. In that office, I was able to become familiar with many families and was able to see how they worked, or didn't work, as the case may be. Those enlightening years even more solidly built my ideas of men as a luxury. I saw so many couples that were so incompatible and unhappy that they literally were frequently sick and sometimes chronically ill from the constant tension and frequency of violence and infidelity. I grieved for these people, these families, and these children being born into such stressful circumstances.

Oftentimes, I knew generations of the same families, their extended families, in-laws, ex in-laws, and I became aware of generations of unhappiness, stress, patterns of dysfunction that I knew were going to be passed down into their innocent beautiful babies that passed through our doors. One of the most unforgettable outrages that still angers me to this day was when a woman that we had not known long brought in a beautiful but very sick child to our office. I asked who this lovely child was and was stunned to hear, "this is the step kid that I got stuck with."

I honestly do not know how I exited that room peacefully. Another generation of dysfunction, another child who would grow up and just want someone to love him and would, and probably did, fish in the wrong pond. I truly wish that I knew where that child is today.

I also saw generations of families who were truly, beautifully bonded together with love, respect, and hope for the future. They welcomed their new babies with exhilaration, regardless of how much money was in the bank account or in their wallets. New life was new hope, a new adventure. These grandparents supported their children in life and love. Through their interactions, they taught their children how to love, cherish, and raise their own children into respectful, well-balanced, well-loved adults. I loved keeping up with these families. A trip to the doctor for stitches or even a 103-degree temperature was also an opportunity for them to share all about their children, grandchildren, and sometimes even great grandchildren. This is probably one of the greatest things I took away from nursing when I chose to leave it. It certainly guided my next step in career choice.

Although my own family certainly is not without dysfunction, there was always this love, this strength of believing in nourishing the family and bringing peace, safety, and love to the children, some of whom were born to us and some of whom were acquired (and no one in my family is or ever has been a "step kid," much less one we got stuck with).

I have to share the best parenting advice I ever was graced with. It was not eloquently stated, but it was absolutely eloquent in its simplicity and it is solidity in starting and maintaining an emotionally healthy person whom, at a later date, will naturally move toward finding a luxury of their own lives.

When I was pregnant with my first child, I was very nervous. At lunch at my grandmother's house one day, I was sharing my anxieties with her. She simply said, "rock 'em till you can't get up with 'em anymore." This was her advice, nothing about bathing, feeding, sickness or juggling…just rock 'em till you can't get up with the anymore. At first, I thought she had lost her mind, but as I was driving around the community working home health, memories began running through my head and my heart.

I was a small child from the outset. My parents were in the midst of a rough marriage, which ultimately ended in divorce, and I was born at a bad time. My grandmother cared for me a large portion of the time when I was young. The memories of her rocking me came flooding in, rocking me when I was cradled in her arms as a small child. Rocking me as I lay in her lap with my head on her shoulder. Finally, rocking me with my head on her shoulder and my chest against hers with my feet through the arms of the chair touching the ground…she couldn't get up with me anymore, so we napped together.

This is a luxury of love so strong that it cements a foundation of love and belonging into one's soul that nothing can destroy. This is the foundation that we all need to start out our journey in life toward, that time that we truly know our soul, our self. And when we are ready to find a luxury to share that life, that self with, we will find it. I experienced this within my own family, even amidst the craziness. I also witnessed it in the office where I worked. I did encounter and witness love and respect within the families that passed this love down generation to generation, just as mine did. And still today, I meet extensions of these families that were not even a twinkle in someone's eye when I knew their forefathers back in that little office years ago. More often than not, they tell me how their great grandparents, grandparents, and parents are doing. I see how, from the examples that these fine family members set, they have moved on and are married or getting married, carrying babies on their hips, and I have no doubt that it will all be fine.

When my first child was born, I did exactly as grandma had told me; I rocked and rocked and rocked. My second was born seventeen months later. Let me tell you; it's hard to rock two babies at once, but I mastered it, and the person doing the rocking experiences the same peace, love, and sense of belonging as those babies being rocked do. Today, as I sit here typing from my home office in our empty nest, we both know our two grown children are emotionally healthy, productive members of society and will nurture their own lives and their luxury in and of life.

Yes, my career in nursing taught me so much. Even watching the day to day relationship of the doctor that I worked for and his beloved wife taught me so much about cooperation and support. Nursing both in home health and office nursing gave me further evidence that families are built and nurtured from two people who have defined themselves first, and then searched for a person who would be their luxury in life. Nursing made my idea stronger. However, the time came when I wanted to further my career, and I went back to college as a nontraditional student with two kids and a husband who was, at that time, an over the road truck driver. What to do, what to do? That is a big decision when you are registering as an adult who is beating herself up for not getting it right the first time and who feels she is wasting her children's time. Initially, I chose teaching, a choice by default.

Being a nontraditional student is hard. It is hard for the kids and for the poor, unsuspecting husband who had no clue what was about to befall our household. But being the luxury, he is, he dug in his heels, hung on, and learned not to talk to me during midterms and finals. He also learned that an empty wine bottle in the trash meant there was a Spanish test tomorrow.

Soon, I realized I was taking more social work classes than education classes and switched majors. Neither my husband nor my daddy was happy about that one, but they respected and supported me. I had found my niche. The off-handed comment I had made to my young daughter throughout the years was now not only gaining strength from life experience. It was gaining solid theory and a wonderful knowledge base…and it kept slowly expanding in my head.

Even more clearly with the training in social work and psychology that I would eventually achieve, I could see so many flaws, poor decisions that seemed to be keeping people down and unhappy. I saw a lot of people getting caught in infidelity. I saw a lot of parents who weren't fulling enjoying and parenting their children effectively.

Angry and unhappy people with, what I know to be now, somatic complaints might have had headaches or belly aches that somehow doctors could never diagnose. As I had worked for that wonderful doctor, I observed and stored all kinds of information and thoughts. Many afternoons I traveled from home to college and back with the radio cranked as loud as it would go and felt my heart and soul ache for people while my brain tried to sort it all out.

As the years flew by, I finished my degree in Social Work…wow. The career that the social work degree brought really opened my eyes! Enter Child Welfare. Child Welfare rapidly and savagely opens your eyes, strengthens your beliefs, and (excuse me) gives you balls of steel. This is where the book probably really set in motion. I encountered family after family, so many issues, so many horrible family traditions and cycles of abuse. Every situation, if tracked back, linked back to a poor choice in a mate and a poor expectation of what a relationship should be. Holy cow, this was an experience!

During my years of child welfare, I learned so much. My heart also hurt more during that time than any other in my life. The education I got there about life cycles, abuse, neglect, dysfunction, and love was equivalent to nothing I can explain. I would not change those years for anything. As hard as it was, it was also an adventure that taught me so much of the world and showed me things about family that I thought I comprehended, but in reality, only had a small idea of like the vast cycles of dysfunction that life can turn into. I met and interacted daily with families that had been in cycles of abuse and dysfunction for so long and so many generations that they truly could not comprehend what, if anything, about life that could be a luxury. They had no belongingness, no expectation of love or the expectation that their needs would be met. They surely could not envision a luxury of any kind.

I also witnessed enormous family love and strength, and goals. Nothing feels better than reuniting children with their family after you have taken them from their parents. I worked in the trenches to rebuild a family and then reunite them. I have witnessed, and during that time, learned the strength of humanity and personal family perseverance.

There are a few families that will always be a part of my heart, soul, and of my history. They were my greatest teachers of that time period of my life. One of my very first forays into "picking up" children was very traumatic. I remember clearly at the end of it all, somewhere around 2 or 3 a.m., my brand-new boss was following me around the whole building begging me not to quit. Yes, it was that bad. And I have to be honest, all the while I was telling her that I wasn't going to quit, I really wanted to. That decision that I made that night to stick it out was based solely on one thing. I had made a promise to that mother earlier in the day that I would stick it out with her and she would not have to endure yet another change in case workers. That same woman was in jail that night for trying to assault me while her children were being taken from her home. I didn't blame her and was not in the least bit angry with her. In fact, that desperate lunge she took at me that got her hauled off was truly the only shred of hope that I had that this family would be restored. Everything else pointed to the children never going home and the parents wasting away on drugs. I stayed because I made her a solemn promise, but I had almost no hope that the family would rebound.

That family, however, truly taught me the most valuable lesson in humanity and family love that I have learned to date. They took a while to restore themselves to who they truly were. I was, and still am, amazed at what wonderful people emerged and how they fought tooth and nail for their children. That family was restored within a year. That family is still intact today with more generations to love. I am still in contact with them and hope to always be. That family taught me that no matter what the obstacles, even if the biggest obstacle is one's self, it can be overcome. People can come out of the deepest void and become wonderful, loving, emotionally healthy, beautiful people. I have been given the privilege of witnessing this many, many times. I am so grateful to that first family that showed this to me.

Tying this back to luxury, even if one has lived through generations of abuse, dysfunction, and chaos, he or she can restructure the environment, build a support system, learn healthy communication, build self-esteem and worth, and ultimately become whole enough to seek and find a luxury, thus breaking a vicious cycle.

I honestly have to say that during this time, I was learning so much about how families functioned and did not function, so at that time, I was not thinking of writing a book at some point. Instead, I was hanging on like hell for the ride and soaking in what that entire ride had to teach. At the end of my days of child welfare, though, I left with no regrets, a wealth of knowledge, faith, and some heartache. I exited the building a much wiser person than when I had entered. Of course, I left for school, and everything I had learned pointed me toward the real goal. I wanted to be a therapist. I remember watching *M\*A\*S\*H* growing up and how my favorite character, other than Hawkeye, was Sidney Freedman, the traveling psychiatrist. I thought he had the coolest job in the world. I just didn't know that kind of work was something you could learn to do. Thank goodness, I figured it out. I'm not a psychiatrist, though, but a therapist. I get to see people day to day, week to week. Since I entered the world of a therapist, the book thing has never been far from my mind.

I have never been more convinced that the paradigm shift that could eliminate my job security is, in fact, "Men are a Luxury, not a Necessity." And I would be quite happy to retire if that were to eliminate my job. I would feel very confident to say that 99% of my clients are in one way or another going through whatever conflict they present to me because of poor choices concerning marital and family incongruence.

I have been very blessed in my career choices. I have learned an innumerable amount of life lessons. I have a tremendously large, hilarious, imperfect, "dysfunctional" family that has more love and strength of bond holding it together than I could have ever imagined. I have two beautiful children that have grown up in this family to be healthy productive wonderful people who have found their luxuries and are now bringing me grandbabies to "rock 'em till I can't get up with 'em." These grandchildren have been welcomed and will be raised in the most loving family possible. My luxury and I are very proud of both our successes and our failures, because both brought us to where we are today.

I am at a point now that I have experienced and learned enough to finally share my proposal for a paradigm shift with others. Men are a Luxury, not a Necessity. Please do not misunderstand me; I am in no way at the end of my life lessons and adventures. I will continue to live, love, and grow each and every day that I live and breathe because that is the greatest lesson that my momma taught me.

I have worked on this book in sporadic fits of frenzy. I have put it aside and pondered. I have struggled with self-esteem issues surrounding writing this book. I am back at it again for the long haul. A couple of weeks ago, my luxury told me that I needed to get up off it and go back to writing because he could tell that my brain was bored and needed to be productive. He further elaborated the fact that he felt that I was either going to go back to college for another degree or finish this book. He stated ostentatiously that the world needs this book, but also that he doesn't think he has it in him to endure another adventure through college with me. He knows me so well, and himself. Also, during all the years, I have been pondering, starting and stopping this book, my children have grown up. My son is a therapist himself working at Arkansas State University counseling center. He has found his luxury, and they have blessed us with a granddaughter. My daughter has found her luxury and has a Master's in English and teaches college. Her luxury is also an English teacher. What two better colleagues to see Vonda and me through this project? You will be meeting them and seeing their influence through the editing process. My luxury and I are truly blessed. I am also truly blessed to have traveled many roads with my dear friend Vonda.

# Brokenness Versus Wholeness

Often you hear women talking of the person to whom they are engaged, married or dating. Just as often, they tell you as much about what is "wrong" with them as they tell you what is "right" with them. Just as often, you watch their relationship from afar and fear or dread begins to build in your gut. It is like watching a train wreck in slow motion. You want to stop it, or at the very least, look away and pray it doesn't come to fruition. You cannot seem to look away or stop it, though. It is, after all, their mistake to make

Often this sense of anxiety comes from the expectations you know they have about the way they are going to "change, or whip their partner into shape," to turn them into what they desire their partner to be. They are buying a necessity hoping it will turn into a luxury. Why? Does your old beater car ever materialize into a swanky Mercedes Benz with butt heaters just because you want it to? Of course not. Again, luxury versus necessity. You need a car and any car that gets you from point A to point B is sufficient. If we are talking luxury, however, you want those butt warmers to work, the paint to shine, and the engine to purr like a kitten. You want it to feel not only purposeful but luxuriously at peace in that mechanical art, and it doesn't matter if it costs more to fill it up and it gets virtually no gas mileage, it's a luxury, not a necessity. You're looking for that feeling that immediately permeates my soul when I sit down at that little bar in Cozumel. Luxury. This woman will take a day at the beach over a Mercedes any day of the week.

If that man is going to be a luxury in your life, bottom line, he has to give more positives to the relationship than the amount of energy that you have to input to "make it work" or to "train him." He is an addition to your life, not a child you've taken to raise. Many people feel they need to be a part of a relationship and probably have not even thought about what they want a relationship to be. They most likely stumbled into someone with pretty eyes, a nice smile, or some other relatively shallow trait which they find attractive. That person in turn sees something equally shallow or narrowly defined about them...soon an attachment is formed. And the snowball is heading down the hill getting bigger and bigger and more out of control.

They aren't thinking about how this person will fit into their lives; instead they are thinking, "I have to have somebody to prove there is nothing wrong with me." So, they stay with the cute eyed guy, trying to contort, cajole, threaten, and forcibly press him into a mold that was defined by someone else. The problem here is obvious. You can't change someone who doesn't want to change. Furthermore, if you feel the need to change who they actually are, you either are not happy with them or with yourself. So, you have been fishing in the wrong pond, caught a catfish when you wanted a trout. The catfish will do. It will give the appearances that you have caught the prize, done the work, and fulfilled your obligation. But if your heart desires trout almandine, fried catfish is not going to fit the bill long-term. And no, you can't turn a catfish into a trout. There is nothing wrong with a catfish. Some people are just trout people and some people are catfish people. In short, you don't grab some random guy off the street and proceed to mold him into what you want. Men are not clay, and few of us are that artistically talented, and even then, no one but God can build a person. The alternative is to shop more effectively, and you need a list, defined criteria of what constitutes luxury in your life. Mercedes or day at the beach. Trout or catfish. It's your choice. Just be sure you can find a match for your choice.

To be clear, though, before you can even make your lift, you have to "do the work on yourself." In my line of work over the past numerous years, I see so few people who can actually, with clarity, define themselves. If they can't define themselves, how on earth can they define what constitutes a luxury for them? Answer? They don't. They make a choice by default hoping that will define it for them Big Mistake. My mother's first marriage was a choice by default. She wanted out away from her alcoholic father; at that time, the only way to do that was to marry my biological father. He was a very troubled man, and after a massive traumatic event, he became full-fledged mentally ill and ran away.

Her second marriage to my dad has been, and is still, an ongoing adventure. They are soul mates. They took their six kids between them and built one hell of a family. They have loved and respected each other through all the trials and tribulations. They know and accept each other's demons and know how to soothe and help each other fight those demons when they arise. And man, are they still having fun! They recently came back with a very poignant picture that dad had taken of mom posing for him on their balcony of their stateroom on a cruise ship. As he handed me the picture, he said, "your mother is a damn fine-looking woman." They are ninety-two and eighty-three and still having this much fun together. Priceless! They know and are at peace with both themselves and each other.

That being said, let's track the process of growth and human development through Maslow's hierarchy of needs to create human creatures capable of achieving and maintaining the above described bond. We can then identify how this applies to and guides our journey toward self-knowledge and, ultimately, our ability to find luxury in our own lives. At the base of psychology is human development, how a new born evolves into a grown individual with a personality, entrenched morality, emotional stability and a soul. While most theorists identify stages according to age or physical growth, Maslow uses important needs that must be met at each stage in order to seamlessly move to the next level of development. Just like grief is like a rise and fall of waves moving back and forth, Maslow's stages can also do this if the stages are not met in order. Maslow identifies the first stage as physiological needs, food and shelter. This is the basis. If not met, the child will die.

The second stage is safety, both physical and emotional safety. The child's needs are met, and the child comes to rely on the fact that if he cries, a bottle will be presented and his needs will be taken care of. If a child's cries never produce a response, eventually the child will stop crying. Once this stage is stable and the child is thriving, he begins to feel the emotional feelings of love and belonging. We all need to feel like we belong somewhere. It gives us ground to stand on, so to speak. We identify ourselves as belonging to this family and counting on the love and acceptance of this family. If we don't have consistency of these feelings and experiences in this stage, the person will feel socially out of place, unwanted, and may not be able to be in a healthy relationship.

If the person continues through the stages and daily life and all goes well according Maslow, the person will develop self-esteem and self-worth. They understand they are important, valuable people in this world and are confident enough to interact with others on respectful and honest level of communication and interaction. They feel like they deserve relationships and want and look for healthy relationships to continue feeling the love and belongingness they've learned to participate in on other levels.

Once esteem is achieved and maintained, you see a healthy individual who is still growing and thriving. They are moving toward self-actualization, which is a state of feeling and moving through life at a heightened awareness and appreciation of self and others. Self-actualized people are ready to begin to desire a luxury in life in the form of a mate. If people don't receive or achieve what they needed on one or more levels, they will have to backtrack and find ways to learn those social milestones to have cathartic breakthroughs and grow into healthy people. People move at their own pace.

An emotionally healthy adult is expected to be able to live and function effectively within our society and within our subcultures of society. Marriage and family is certainly one of the most important subcultures that individuals are expected to navigate effectively. The family ensures the survival of the species and further development of our species into a more savvy, more advanced version of humanity of past generations.

Adults who are not socially or emotionally healthy are certainly not a lost cause. If given the right environment and support, every human can grow and develop emotional skills that she missed growing up. One can come to terms with trauma, mistakes, and emotional abandonment and grow to an emotionally healthy individual and become ready and willing to become someone's luxury and to accept someone as her luxury.

Basically, even though humans are animals, they have very few instincts left. It then follows that basically all behaviors are learned. Anything that has been learned can be unlearned and relearned or reframed. They can develop healthier goals or even goals that are truer to themselves, not borrowed from someone else. We do tend to follow leads of those who provide positivity in our lives. We connect with these people for support because they provide positivity or acceptance. They make up for things and people that may have been missing earlier. However, again to be clear, this is their own project. Do not see these people as a project for you to create a perfect mate. They are their own project. Leave them be; they're not done yet. We attach to our support systems and feel belongingness and acceptance, and we may utilize them as a spring board that was missing in early life.

Some years ago, I was offered the opportunity to teach a college class, Medical Aspects of Disability, for one semester. I saw this as a wonderful opportunity for personal growth and adventure. So, I embarked on my first semester of teaching. I enjoyed most all the topics of the chapters. All nurses, and doctors for that matter, have at least one area that they cannot stand and hate to deal with. Mine is cardiology. No one could pay me enough to work on the cardiac floor. When that chapter came up, I did the basics of the heart, then asked a guest speaker to come in and share his experience of having a heart attack. I asked my dad to come in. I introduced him by his given name and as my dad. He spoke eloquently, openly with humor and humility. He gave the "down and dirty" of what this experience is like.

As he finished answering questions, he hugged me, told me he loved me, and to be careful driving home. Once he was out the door, I addressed the first hand to fly into the air. Their statement was "Man, you're just like your dad; we would have known he was your dad whether or not you had shared that with us." I asked how many agreed with that statement and every hand shot up. I then revealed that he was and is my dad, but not biologically. I smiled as I watched the shock move over their faces. We had a wonderful talk about nature versus nurture.

Nurture moves us up the stages of self-discovery and ultimately self- acceptance. It certainly advances you easier if you have people to cushion your life, but it doesn't really matter at what age they enter your life. Furthermore, if one doesn't get this at home from family, it can be gained from someone or some event totally unrelated to an individual. Given the opportunity, everyone will grow to a degree, and most will thrive. This is not instinct or genetics; it's learning, and everyone can learn. Everyone, no matter what age, is still writing in their book of life.

I obviously was very blessed with the people in my life that nurtured me through each life event and life stage. Many are not so lucky and have not gained the level of emotional health to become a good luxury at that time in their life. Pay them respect and walk on by. They have to work on themselves. People (who are not dependent on them for anything) can nurture them, mentor them, but down to brass tacks, they have the responsibility of growth to themselves. These people are no lost causes but in the same vein. They are not candidates for a luxury. Be their friend if you have to but only for support. Do not put them in boyfriend or girlfriend role. They simply are not ready. They need personal growth, self-exploration, self-esteem, and worth. They need, perhaps, therapy. They are not luxury material at this time. They are human and are deserving of respect, but not ready to engage in a healthy relationship.

In the mirror perspective, you may be in the same boat. If you cannot maintain a healthy relationship with anyone. If you continually meet and take in people who are controlling, abusive, non-attentive to your life and adventure, you are fishing in the wrong pond. You need to stop fishing for a while and work on you. Go to therapy, explore your feelings, explore your expectations, and explore your communication styles. You're probably not ready to fish. Work on you and who you want to be, who you need to be, for *you*.

Trust, value of life and self, and happiness comes from within.

Many people, who are not emotionally healthy themselves will stumble across these people, feel sorry for them, or develop a "you and me against the world dynamic" and begin a relationship. This is a mistake. Soon, both people will be unhappy, that they don't have the kind of mate they want. Neither are having their expectations met. Soon, one gets offended and defensive because they feel they are giving more than they are getting and nothing is 'right.' Shake hands, thank each other for the happy moments, wish each other well, and move on. Neither of you were ready. Immediately begin work on yourself.

We are all looking for the happy ending. That is a fallacy. Ending? The only real ending is death. It is about the journey toward the ending. The best we can hope for at the ending is that we made the journey count and harbor no regrets or unfinished business. Eriksonian theory has many stages, but the final one being generativity versus stagnation. In plain English, we get to a certain point in our lives where we look back and review our adventure called life. Hopefully, we are at peace with the life we have led. Hopefully, we laugh and give thanks that so many things were so good. Hopefully, we have shared much of the ride with a luxury who was our partner in every aspect. Hopefully, the couple sits together and reminisces and is proud and satisfied at what they've done, AND are still engaging in what they can still do, and they do it. They engage in family, they travel, they go visit friends, and they go out to lunch. Even when knees ache and backs crack, you can and should be still as active in life as possible. My parents are eighty-three and ninety-two and as hilarious as they are beautiful. They have taught me that I want to live up until my dying day.

As stated before, we are a very large family. My mother goes to lunch twice a day, although she only eats once. She chooses a grandchild, child or even great grandchild and picks her up at 11 and takes her to lunch. She takes her back to work at a few minutes until 12 and goes and picks up another and takes her to lunch. This is how she keeps in touch, actively participates in her family's lives. When someone is in college, my dad can tell you his grade point, the number of hours he has behind and ahead of him. He proudly attends graduations. He loves to sit and talk to all his kids. He is proud of each one, even when he is mad at something …stupid or unfortunate …they might have done. He is always right there waiting for whoever walks through the door. This is generativity. They've lived an exciting adventurous life together, and they are still doing everything they can to remain active and engaged.

Stagnation is when an older person looks back and may or not see unfortunate decisions, tragedies they never came to terms with, lethargy, and they become disillusioned and just sit and wait until death comes. This is stagnation. This is a tragedy. This often happens when one has spent a life time with someone that was not their luxury but they just stuck it out for whatever reason. They were unhappy for most of their life, and they will most likely stagnate at the end.

My all-time favorite quote is "Life should not be a journey to the grave with the intention of arriving safely in an attractive and well- preserved body, but rather to skid in sideways, chocolate in one hand, wine in the other, totally worn out, and screaming,

"WoooHooo, what a ride!" This is truly the philosophy of an emotionally healthy individual. If you are one of these emotionally healthy individuals that view life in this way, I bet you have a wonderful luxury skidding right along beside you carrying the corkscrew and the wine glasses!!!

# Of the Self

It may seem strange to address the essence of the self in a book about healthy, luxurious relationships; however, it actually makes perfect sense. If there is no self, there cannot be a couple. Furthermore, the level of emotional health of the self is directionally proportional to the level of health within the relationship. The key is a psychological staple theory: self-actualization.

A healthy self is important to a relationship in that what you bring into the relationship defines what you can give and accept, which is what makes it truly a luxury. When we are healthy emotionally, we begin to crave, search for, and create bonds of friendship within family and intimacy within relationships. And, we have an innate sense of what we want them to bring to our lives and what we want to give them in return. We begin to try our wings in relationships and, most importantly, we value their worth so we feed them and feed *on* them.

Through positive achievement of interaction within relationships, we experiment and further refine and build our self-definition of what we want a relationship to be. We also fine tune our sense of self. Furthermore, we are secure in our knowledge that who we are is a living, breathing, growing creature of God that always has positive values, but always is capable of more growth. We become confident and build higher positive self-esteem. Who we are is valuable, but we are always moving forward through growth and are constantly evolving into a more finely tuned version of who we are and who we are going to be. Positive self-esteem and sense of self grows and blooms in massive proportion and becomes the largest aspect of all products of life. We achieve respect for and value all other human beings and all creations of God.

From this point, we engage fully in community and in the world around us. By achieving self -value, we invest that into value of others and the surrounding world as well. We interconnect; we see and feel the connection of self to the whole of society. We develop morality, sense of responsibility, creativity, and acceptance of life and of the world.

Maslow defines self-actualization as "the state, which is highest of the human needs, involves the active use of all our qualities and abilities, the development and fulfillment of our potential. To become self -actualizing, we must first satisfy the needs that stand lower in an innate hierarchy" (*History of Modern Psychology* 463). Maslow went on to define common characteristics or tendencies of self -actualizing individuals:

1. An objective perception of reality
2. A full acceptance of their own nature
3. A commitment and dedication to some kind of work
4. Simplicity and naturalness of behavior
5. A need for autonomy, privacy and independence
6. Intense mystical or peak experiences
7. Empathy with and affection for humanity
8. Resistance to conformity
9. A democratic character structures
10. An attitude of creativeness and
11. A high degree of what Adler termed social interest (463-464).

If one looks closely at the above list, it can be said that not only are these earmarks of a positive sense of self, but they are also earmarks of a healthy, luxurious relationship. A relationship must exist and thrive in the reality of the world as it truly exists. We have to interrelate to the world both as an individual and as a couple or family unit. This includes engagement in work, purpose, and interconnectedness with the world around us. No individual or couple can exist within a vacuum. We develop the desire, the feeling of responsibility to be a part of something greater than ourselves.

Once we reach this point on an individual level, we are ready to identify criteria for our search for a mate, otherwise known as the ultimate luxury to complement our lives and how our lives interconnect with the world. All does not have to be glitz and glam. We learn to appreciate and value little things in life. We gain joy from simply interacting with the world and or lives on a simple day to day level, and we want someone to share those things, great and small, that give us joy. We do not have to have that person, we can enjoy life as an individual, but we desire that luxury of a companion who compliments our life and shares those feelings of joy and peace.

For me, the big thing is the ocean, my ultimate sense of peace and connectedness is with the ocean. I can sit in Cozumel in that small open-air bar right at the side of the ocean. I can sit there all day in total peace, feeling and smelling the ocean breeze, watching and hearing the waves crash, seeing the ship moored in the harbor and watching the tourists and locals going about their day. When I engage in meditation or in self-hypnosis or even just day dreaming, this is my safe place, my oasis. I can do this alone and still feel the peace in my soul. But to have my luxury by my side enriches the experience. He does not share my love of the ocean to as much of a degree as do I, but he loves to share my joy at being there. Enrichment of my life brings enrichment to his and vice versa.

As for the small things, the day to day, because most of us cannot live on the seashore every day, we also have to feel joy and a sense of purpose and interconnectedness in our everyday routines. We can do this on our own, but the experience is richer if we have a well fitted luxury to enrich it with. Work is a sense of joy and pride within us, even on bad days, because we gain part of our definition of self through "what we do." If you think about it, it is one of the first questions we ask new acquaintances and one of the first things we share about ourselves. It is an intricate part of our lives. By conquering this personal task, we more clearly define ourselves and thus more clearly define who would be a fitting addition to our lives based on sharing this part of ourselves.

We have to respect and support our mate's commitments as we expect our own to be respected and supported. In addition, we want to share this very large part of ourselves with someone. And we want that some one to respect, admire, and believe in what we do, whether or not they share the same vocation. My husband has always supported my choice of careers, but he hasn't always been, and sometimes still is not happy, about my choices. He, and my dad, hated me being in child welfare. My husband is at peace with therapy. He still worries about me though, but respects and has come to believe that although many of my clients are not stable, I am, and I know what I am doing.

As a therapist, even though I cannot share any details or specifics about my case load, I can share the philosophy, love, and belief in what I do with my luxury. Even though his vocation is entirely different than what I do, he respects my love of and my dedication to the mental health field, as I respect his field. Couples do not have to have the same careers to be close; careers are part of the characteristics of independence, our own little slice of life that we manage on our own and with our colleagues. Then we go home and share with our luxury to unwind from the stress or to share our sense of purpose when something went really right or really wrong. Again, our mate doesn't define our career. They complement it, and they respect and value it because we do. We have to respect each other's own space and not feel threatened by that space. For most couples, the career is that space where they interact alone and share the outcome and show support for each other's independence and self-definition

# Faith and Spirituality

Religion can bring spouses together or push them apart. When couples are on the verge of a major life transition such as marriage, they begin to think about life, love, values... and the future. To a great extent, this is what spirituality is about- our human search for happiness and the meaning of life. Is life just about the here and now? Do morals make any difference? Is death really the end? Is there a reason to live beyond my own comfort? Is that all there is?

Perhaps you're putting off some of these heavy questions for a rainy day when your job is more settled, or wedding pressures subside...or you reach retirement. Whether you address them or not, however, the big life issues will not disappear. They may go underground until a crisis appears- an accident, a child with a serious illness, or a looming divorce. All of a sudden, you start wondering what the rock is on in which you ground your life. That is the way some people discover their spiritual sides, but you don't have to wait for a crisis. It's so much easier to let faith keep your relationship strong, rather than rescue you in an emergency.

What difference does faith make to a marriage? The time before marriage is an opportunity to take stock of your basic beliefs and values together. Share them with your beloved and chart how you will live out your beliefs and values together. Does this mean you have to share the same faith? That's nice, but it's more important to talk about what God means to you, what spiritual practices you find meaningful, and how you can support each other once you are married. If only one spouse believes that faith is important, how does he or she stay motivated to attend services if the other is sleeping or recreating? It is not impossible, but it is more supportive go to services together.

Research conducted by the Center of Marriage and Family at Creighton University (1999) showed a higher incidence of divorce among interchurch couples (20.3%). Interchurch couples are defined as Christians of different faiths of different denominations being married to each other. Religion can bring couples together or push them apart. Couples may be of different religions, but that alone does not predict marital instability. What is important is whether couples engage in joint religious activities. For example, do they pray together or read the Bible together?

Although research finds that greater religious practice is related to lower rates of divorce, there is not necessarily a causal relationship. It may be that people who are more actively religious are more likely to oppose divorce, or maybe they work harder at their marital relationship. Let's say you are both religious but form different denominations. Perhaps you share spirituality but not a church home. Certainly, some spouses strongly committed to their faith will continue to worship regularly and be active church members, but it is harder to go alone, split financial support, and devote time to two separate congregations.

The solutions to these dilemmas are as unique as the couples who marry. There are some steps than any couple can take, regardless of faith affiliation. Talk with each other about important stuff.

Start with the basics:

1. Who is God for you?
2. What code of ethics guides your life?
3. Do you value weekly worship?
4. What kind of prayer is comfortable and satisfying to you?
5. How important is it that your spouse shares your religious beliefs?
6. Are you lukewarm in your religious commitment and likely to fade away if you have to do it alone?

If you've never practiced a religion, consider giving it a try.

Although becoming more spiritual is a value for anyone, styles of worship vary as much as the unique people that are seeking the meaning of life. Try out more than one place of worship. If the first one doesn't suit you, try again. It is worth the effort.

Visit each other's church/synagogue/mosque.

If each of you belongs to a different faith tradition, learn more about the beliefs of that religion. You're not trying to convert the other but to understand what shapes your partner's values. (Vonda's experience) My husband and I made the decision before we married that we would be a two-church family. I belonged to The Reorganized Church of Jesus Christ of Latter Day Saints, and he belonged to the United Methodist Church up the hill from our house. But as a two-church family, we decided that we would attend each other's churches together alternating Sundays. We sang in two church choirs and participated in two young adult classes.

If you are getting married in a religious ceremony, use this opportunity. If you are getting married in a religious setting, it means that faith is important to at least one of you. Use this opportunity to discuss questions of faith with your spiritual leader. These are the kind of conversations you may have intended to explore someday, but you've put it off. Now your life is about to change. Use your contact with the priest, minister, rabbi, or imam to go deeper.

Become a grown-up person of faith.

Often people are raised in a religious home. They attend religious education classes and maybe even Catholic or other religious schools for eight, twelve, or sixteen years. But their faith formation got stuck in childhood. If you have grown distant from the faith of your childhood, check it out again on an adult level. If you were a lawyer or doctor, you wouldn't think of practicing your profession based on high school information. Update your knowledge on your faith. You don't have to have a degree in theology, but you should not rely on childhood explanations in and adult world.

Make your home a place of unity.

Even if the two of you come from different faith traditions and are committed to continuing them, make your home a place where you merge prayer, rituals, and religious traditions. Since prayer at home is less formal, you can develop creative, inclusive times of prayer and faith devotions together. Experiment with the rituals of each other's faith and blend them to fit your family. The point is not whose church you go to, but rather that you bring it all home.

I have friends who have been married for almost 40 years. He is Jewish, she is Catholic, and they have made it a practice in their home and with their family to share the traditions of both religions, to attend Christmas and Easter mass together and to be a synagogue for the High Holidays of the Jewish faith. Their six boys attending with them are being encouraged to learn as much as they can about their parents' faiths but are to be allowed to make their own choices about what to practice or not to practice as they became older teens and now as adults.

Do not wait until you have a child to talk about religion.

It is tempting to put off decisions about how you will share your faith (or ignore it) until you have your first child. DON'T! A child is too important to become a battleground. If faith is important to you, discuss how each of you wants to share your faith with any children you may have *before* you are married. If you are Catholic or doing premarital counseling, this question will be part of your marriage preparation. Discussing how you will raise your children can clarify how committed each of you are to your faith and beliefs.

## The Sacrament of Marriage

Marriage is so much more than a license, a ceremony, and a promise made with symbolic jewelry. Marriage is the spiritual union of two souls who have been guided to each other to serve the highest good and create a spiritual family. The exchange of vows is a sacred rite of passage whose true meaning has escaped so many. When the ideals and fantasy of what you think marriage should be and feel like begin to fade, and the realities of responsibility set in, your emotional and spiritual health may take a back seat, and divorce may seem an attractive option to stop the fights and end the suffering.

If your marriage is in trouble and you're starting to doubt the decisions you've made, take a step back and take a breath. Close your eyes and remember that there is always somewhere to turn when you feel you've lost your way. Remember your faith, in any form it comes. Faith will give you strength and clarity and help you change your mind, body, and spirit to one that attracts the experience that you want.

So how do you find the faith to keep your marriage strong?

Here are three ways:

1. Believe in each other.
   a. Finding faith in a partner who has let you down can be painful and difficult. You two may spend so much of your energy trying to fix each other that you forget to believe in and trust in each other. But how can you trust someone who doesn't seem to be changing for the better, or putting in the work that makes the relationships work?
   Believe that your spouse can be different, whether you see the changes or not. Instead of focusing on the missteps of the past, or the fruition of the present, believe that your spouse has the ability to be everything he or she strives to be. And this is the key. Believe that your spouse can uphold his or her own standards or the standards of a higher power, not just yours. No two people are the same. And even in a same faith union does not mean that you and your spouse share identical values or principles in every aspect, nor would those same ideals manifest in identical ways. Find out exactly what your partner thinks and feels about all aspects of marriage, its meanings, and its manifestations. Then believe that it will all happen. And in the meantime, do this same thing for yourself.
2. Believe in your marriage.
   Your marriage is an ordained expression of the lessons of your spiritual system. You and your spouse were brought together to achieve something momentous, and this was not done lightly or in vain. The entity that you, your spouse, and you higher power created is larger than the two of you, more than the sum of its parts. But with great power comes

great responsibility. Upholding your spiritual tenants in the face of everyday adversity becomes paramount in raising your family in the grace and omnipresence of your higher power. Keeping your faith means looking beyond the temporary, the mundane, and the obstacles in your physical and spiritual success. Believe in your marriage as you believe in your higher power and its plans for both of you. Find or rediscover the purpose you two are meant to fulfill together and model that for your children. Teach them to search for the meaning in life's difficulties and the divine in their marriages.

3. Believe in your path.

Your marriage is a milestone on your life long journey to happiness and peace. In matrimony, your road has merged with the road of another, and you are sharing this sacred space as a part of both of your journeys. Marriage is an intersection that you can barrel through, missing the signals and likely causing a collision. Or, you can slow down and usher the other passengers to their destinations. -your spouse and children. Your path took the twists and turns it was meant to, even when you found yourself feeling lost and unguided. You may not have the map, but the right road is the road that you are on, and you and spouse are travelling in the same direction. Travel together. You may need to breathe some fresh air at a rest stop, but use that time to recharge, regroup, and reunite with yourself, your spouse, and your higher power. You and your life mate crossed paths as a way to guide you both home. See your marriage as a vehicle that was created to help you become your true self and find your inner power strength and love.

My husband and I come from parents who were married for decades, my parents for fifty-five years and his for almost sixty-eight. Were their marriages perfect? By no means, but they had some things in common. They believed that marriage was a commitment to each other "till death do you part," and they took their vows to each other under God very seriously. They were grounded in their faith and regularly attended church. They were committed to their families and accepted each other's family as their own. They loved each other through all stages of life and presented a united front even when they certainly didn't agree on everything.

The key to keeping faith and avoiding divorce is not to avoid divorce; it is to thrive in marriage. Really be as fully invested in your marriage as you are in your faith. Believe in it. Trust in it. Know it will guide you and protect you. Remind yourself of how far you've come and how much you've already overcome. Look forward to how far there is to go and how much more there is to experience. And consider how you got here and why you came in the first place. Then let go, and let faith guide the rest of your journey through marriage, family, and life.

# Vonda's Journey

My journey to wholeness and the finding of my luxury is significantly different than that of Nena. We are, after all, individuals and started at different places. Raised by both birth parents who were married fifty-seven years until my father's death, my family was significantly dysfunctional. My mother had been a sexual abuse victim in her family of origin, was fostered by her aunt and uncle, and we were told as children that the reason she lived with them instead of her parents was because her parents had too many children, that they could not afford them. Since Aunt and Uncle could not have kids, she went to live with them.

My mother and dad met during her senior year and married shortly after her graduation. By the time they were married six years, they had three children and often found themselves struggling both financially and emotionally. Both had a difficult time understanding child growth and development and were excessive in their use of physical discipline. Fortunately, they had my father's parents and my mother's aunt and uncle who helped when they could.

My favorite memories at my grandparents' home was listening to my Irish grandmother tell me stories about the fairies that lived in the garden and the leprechauns that made the rocking chair squeak and the bread rise, her rocking me and singing to me, teaching me to do an Irish jig. I remember smells of my grandfather's carpentry shop, playing in the saw dust, and having him swing me up on his shoulder, his chewing tobacco that made me sick as a dog when I tried it just like grandpa, the sounds of the Detroit Tigers on the radio, or the sounds of the Green Valley Jamboree on the tv.

At my Aunt and Uncle's, I heard Uncle tell stories of when he fought the Indians or traveled by covered wagon across the plains, all this from a city boy who grew up in Toledo, who teased my brother about "Jojo the dog faced boy" who was supposed to live out in the shed. My German uncle would pour us little shots of beer when we were children and no one thought anything about it. He smelled like machine shop and old spice and had come of age during "the roaring 20's", he loved women in short hair that were smart and shared their opinions. From Aunt, I experienced the gentle hands and voice of a woman who dried my tears, bandaged my booboos, and told me she would hold me on her lap until I was twenty-one. Someone who sewed me clothes for my dolls, helped us set of a tent of an old blanket thrown over the clothes line. She taught us how to make wreathes and necklaces out of dandelions, taught us how to make hollyhock blossoms into dancers in the sink, and told us about our family history when we took flowers to the cemetery.

Sexual abuse was not talked about in our family, and when I was raped at age nine, I had no real understanding of what was happening to me. When told not to tell because my father would go to prison, I believed him. The effects of sexual abuse were long lasting and invasive. Children exposed to sexual touch are often confused by what might have felt funny or even pleasurable. More often, they are very confused by the attention given to them by the abuser.

Abusers seek out children who are lonely or needy, or children who are convenient. This man was closely tied to our family. For years after the rape, he would catch me alone while my family was visiting with them and cop a feel or take a kiss and remind me never to tell. And for years, I didn't.

Those years were spent confused and fearful of this horrible secret that I had. This secret that made me feel like I was different, like there was something wrong with me. By the time my mother talked to me and my younger sister about periods and how that allowed a woman to have a baby, I had not been an innocent for four years. Since then, I have learned that one out of seven girls and one out of twenty-five boys have experienced things similar as to what I had experienced.

One of the things that early sexual abuse often does is set that child up for other sexual abuse or for sexual activity at a young age. For me, by the time I was a teenager, I was sexually active and often times engaged in risky sexual behavior. I had begun think that I had no control or choice about what I did sexually or who I engaged in sexual activity with.

On the other side of the sexually abused Vonda was the Vonda who had been exposed to church and faith at a young age. My parents ran hot and cold about church with either being in church every time the doors were open or only there on Christmas, Easter, and Bible school until we move to my mother's home town, where Aunt and Uncle lived when I was in the tenth grade.

Then we were not only in church every time the doors opened, but on Tuesday night, my mother would take a car load of kids to a meeting called WEY, Witnessing Enthusiastic Youth. It was a group that included sitting on the floor, singing to guitars, and prayers and testimonies. It was here that I heard someone say for the first time that they "were a creation of God and that God didn't create junk." For the first time, I thought, "Really? Even me"?

The struggle for wholeness began there in the basement of Union Church in Grand Rapids Michigan. Let me tell you, that spark didn't change my sexual behavior. It took years and a great deal of work for me to get past my sexual behavior and the sexual abuse that started it. I had worked hard on nurturing that spark that I had found all those years ago. I had made such significant progress on how I felt about myself and how I had dealt with the sexual issues of my childhood. Through this work, I came to realize that there were other things in my childhood that also affected me.

The death of my beautiful Irish grandmother when I was ten and the estrangement of my father from my grandfather tore my heart out. These two men's stubbornness affected the grandchildren who no longer belonged.

At seventeen, I lost the most precious woman who promised to hold me until I was twenty-one. She died of leukemia. In addition to the horrible grief I felt in my childhood, in my working on myself, I came to understand that my mother's hitting you with whatever was convenient, even if it was a belt, a broom, a hair brush or my brother's hot wheels track, had left emotional scars...but for me it was the belief that when my mother was mad at me, when she was yelling or hitting, that she didn't love me. Let me say again that it was my *BELIEF* that my mother didn't love and not the fact that she didn't love me.

44

She did and still does love my sister, brother, and me, but my mother was a product of sexual abuse in the early 1940's when children were seen and not heard and where families "just handled these things." In my mother's case, she went to live with Aunt and Uncle. My grandfather's sister who had been molested when she was a teenager stepped in to protect my mother when Mother told her what was happening, and I suspect it was with the message that, "you are ok now, and "we don't talk about these things."

My mother loved us, but I think she sometimes felt trapped by us. Maybe she felt that she had given up the possibility of a career in music to be a wife and mother. She has, over the years, used her creative talents to offer private music lessons, to substitute teach in public school, and to work in a recreation program in Tucson that has taught numerous Sunday School, Bible School, and Camp classes. However, she had never been given the recognition she might have received if she had been able to pursue her music as a career.

In the years before I met my luxury, I had experienced significant heartbreak from fishing in polluted ponds and from jumping into relationships that didn't have a chance in hell of working. This self-destructive behavior had reached an explosive point, and it was during a horrible argument with my parents that I shared that I had been raped as a child by my parents' best friend. In turn, my mother shared that she had been molested in her family of origin at an early age.

That horrible fight didn't keep me from continuing with my self-destructive behavior, but it did lay out in the open those long-kept family secrets. Now deceased, my mother had flashbacks of rape and abuse on her deathbed, as he daughters held her and told her that they forgave for the things that had hurt us growing up and then had to ask that she be sedated to stop the flashbacks.

During the estrangement from my parents due to some relationship choice I had made, I came to realized that many of my relationships I had had over the years had been emotionally abusive and manipulatives ones and I wanted something different, something better.

I sought out my strained relationship with my Heavenly father to find my way back. In turn, I also tried to heal my relationship with my parents. Over the course of the following year, I made a want list in my head and a list that I brought to God in prayer every night.

45

My List

1. I wanted a man that believed in God.
2. I wanted a man who could accept my past.
3. I wanted a lover, a friend.
4. I wanted a companion for my life time.

I made a decision during this time that often seems difficult but was important to the healing of myself. I became celibate. Not only was I not having sex with anyone; I wasn't putting myself in those situations where I have known in the past that it was too difficult to say no. I did not date or hook up with someone at work. I did not visit the bars or clubs. I worked on me. I joined a gym, I went to church, and I went to church camp. I started working at the nursing home. I took care of the needs of others as I allowed myself to heal. And then I started roller skating.

Kerry (my luxury of 35 years) and I met while roller skating. I was working as the Activities Director/Social Work designee (I know, a mouthful of a title, but honestly it was the social work designee part that lead me to going to work at the local DHS office in the child welfare section, that ultimately led to a degree in social work and Master's in Marriage and Family Therapy). I went skating every Thursday night on adult night at the local roller rink.

I will be honest and tell you that after fifteen months, I was looking for someone who met that list that I had developed and prayed over. I will also be honest and tell you that in violation of one of those rules we have talked about, I went home with him on the first night. I don't know if it was the fifteen months of no sex or the slick lines of, "we don't have to do anything, I just like holding you," but I felt a connection.

He was a dad with custody of his son, an officer in the National Guard, and active member of his church. As fantastic as the love making was, the conversation was even better. We talked about our families, and we talked about our churches and why, as adults, we chose to attend church. He shared with me the love he had for his son and that he had remarried his ex-wife so he could be with his son.

I said to myself, "oh crap, he is still married." He then shared with me that she was living with someone, but it was really over. I drove myself home after he took me back to my car, first introducing me to his son at the baby sitter. I had all these thoughts running through my head. "What have you done? What were you thinking? Oh God, he made me feel so wanted! You idiot; you aren't on birth control, and he didn't use anything either!"

As I was mentally beating myself up, I was thinking about how much I liked this guy and how I hoped I was not imagining something. I can tell you, now that it all worked out, that we kept seeing each other and that he filed for divorce February 15. It was final March 15, and we were married May 21, all in 1983. However, what I really want to talk about is the very hard work we have done to keep this marriage together and to have the life we have made together.

First, we have kept God in the center of our family. In our life together from two different Christian denominations, we made a plan initially that we would be a two-church family. We rotated churches each week for almost two years. We sang in choirs of both and had our family picture taken for his church directory, participated in Easter Sun Rise services with his church and Easter 11:00 service with mine. We helped with two Bible schools and grew together in our faith and in or love.

Second, we focused on family and blending our family together. Two months after our first anniversary, I gave birth to our daughter, and we thought at that time that our family was complete. He was there beside me when my little brother (6'4,275 pounds, but he was still my little brother, the one I had mom bring to show and tell to kindergarten was born) when he was killed suddenly in an accident. I was devastated, my husband was with me every step of the way. During this time, I had gone back to school as a social work major and worked as a therapeutic foster care for emotionally disturbed children. A year after my brother's death we had taken in a baby girl that her mother had aged out of foster care and she lived in a travel trailer in our yard when she had no place else to live. The baby's mom knocked on our bedroom door the first night and handed me the screaming baby that she could not get to calm down. Little did we know that we would adopt that baby girl we had grown to love nine months after she had come into our home. Twelve years later we took guardianship of a severely disabled fourteen-year-old foster daughter.

I am a step mom, a birth mom and a foster mom. I am a mother in law and even a former mother in law. My kids are my kids and we have blended together a unique family. They are like most families, they don't always get along but they know that we are proud of them and want the best for them.

During this time, our families of origin continued to be important to us. We would go for the weekend to my parent's home on the river where they moved shortly before our marriage. For several years before my brother died and my parents moved back to Michigan. We had two Thanksgivings, one at noon with my husband's mother's family at the Phelps family reunion and then evening Thanksgiving dinner at my folks'. We continue to spend as much time with extended family as possible, and that includes our children and their families and the children of our hearts, individuals we had adopted into our family

Over the years, we have shared our home with several individuals who, at that same time, needed a place to live and as a result, they have become part of our extended family: individuals who were suddenly homeless, individuals we worked with or were friends with. For the first year of our adopted daughter's life, we shared our home with a young woman with an infant son and pregnant with another. Her husband, a former foster child I had worked with, was in prison and she had no family in the area. She lived with us taking care of our little girl who had been left with us with our custody or guardianship. She enriched our lives and became a part of our extended family. Twenty-five years later, we maintain a relationship with her and their family.

Recognizing the worth of each person we come in contact with, being willing to reach out to others and include them in our lives, has been an important part of our relationship as partners in this thing called marriage.

Over the years, we have availed ourselves of professional help available in our community. It is often a difficult decision to make to enter therapy. We have to recognize that things aren't going as good as we think they should. That I'm (or a family member) not happy, that what I'm doing isn't working. Maybe I feel like my partner isn't listening to me. Therapy allowed me to have a safe place where I could share my fears, my feelings, and my concerns. It taught me listening skills and how to communicate more effectively. It brought my luxury and I back together on the same page as parents and as partners.

Our son, the boy who I met for the first time the night when his dad picked him up at the baby sitters, married and made us grandparents to a granddaughter for the first time over 21 years ago. Twenty months later we were honored to become grandparents to our first grandson. We lost this beloved grandson ten years later to leukemia, three days after his tenth birthday.

Our birth daughter and her husband (who gave us a grandson when they married) have given us four beautiful granddaughters, the next to the youngest being stillborn, to have to bury two granddaughters has had a profound effect of on us. While we tried to support our children in their grief, we supported each other in our own grief. This is an important of being a luxury.

Our son has remarried and brought two wonderful sons into the family when he remarried.

Our adoptive daughter has given us a beautiful active granddaughter and recently remarried into the family, that we haven not yet gotten to meet.

Although our foster daughter will never give us grandchildren, she has been a wonderful playmate for our grandchildren throughout the years. She has given us more love and the privilege to have her forever.

Sometimes we were in family therapy, three different times over the course of twenty years. Sometimes we did marital therapy in addition to family therapy, and once I was in therapy myself dealing with the grief of losing a job I loved and a whole lot of other stuff. Of course, having been in the mental health field for thirty years, I have had some wonderful colleagues who were therapists that have been supportive and encouraging. I have some wonderful colleagues who were supportive and encouraging who held me up when we lost our grandson. They encouraged me to go back to school for my masters in marriage and family therapy.

# Holes in our Souls

Maslow's ultimate goal of his hierarchy of needs is self actualization. It is postulated and probably absolutely true that very few people reach true self-actualization. Our goal is to get as close as we can to create a whole, human soul with peace and self-worth. To get as close as possible, an individual will be at peace with self, others, and the world at large. They will be, for the most part, happy, content people who have a drive to be involved and belong in family, groups, community, and the world at large.

Some people are fortunate enough to be born into a nurturing family environment or have at least a smattering of people in their life to set one on the right path. In a perfect world, that one would then grow smoothly through the stages into a self-actualized adult ready to find a luxury for a mate and move through their life according to their plans.

The rub, being, we do not live in a perfect world. Things can happen at any age and stage that leave a hole in our soul. We can coat that hole like a clam coats a piece of sand to sooth the rub. We do not, however, create pearls. We create something that theoretically looks like Swiss cheese. The edges are smooth, but the hole remains. In essence, it is a scar on our soul.

It creates grief in all its glory of pain and confusion. It does this even if your perfect luxury is by your side holding your hand and doing their best to comfort you and to knit the hole back together for you or with you. Often that is their first response; they love you, and they want to fix it. The problem there is that some holes are necessary evils that belong in our souls. As much as we try to fight, bite, and claw our way to the source of the hole to make it like it was, the hole is still there and always will be. It remains with a sort of mother of pearl /paper machete patch that holds the memories of what caused the hole. Its patchwork appearance in our soul marks an important spot, a spot of love, turned to pain, turned to memories, turned to tentative peace. In that context, it remains. It is twofold in that it can bring both extreme pain and extreme joy when jostled to awareness. It never, however, heals completely. If it did, that important part of our life would just cease to exist from the point it ended and none of us want that.

God made fallible beings. We are not perfect and are not capable of perfection. Neither, by the way, is our luxury. When something with the power to make a hole in our soul happens, both our self and our luxury are initially flopping like fish out of water. We are talking devastation of the soul, not a hangnail. Few are lucky enough to get to adult hood without experiencing holes in our soles.

I would say that even with the early chaos in my life, I was lucky enough. We had just enough dysfunction to focus on the fun part of dysfunction and two parents working like the devil to build a family that would stay together. They succeeded, and I grew up in a loud, hilarious, but deeply loving and loyal family. We had chaos and we had problems, but my parents never gave up, and the result is a beautiful large family of deeply loyal commitments.

I had the early holes of predictable nature. The loss of first love. The loss of my Grandma was a big one. There is still a hole there that mostly emits positive feelings of love, respect, and warmth. The pain of the loss faded years ago. She was ninety- five years old, and I had her well into my adulthood. She got to see my children born and toddle around. We had no issues in our relationship, and it was a completely positive relationship. I was there when she died, and I saw the peace wash over her. It was time.

Some holes are exceptionally painful and when they come like a waterfall. They knock the peace out of you for a while. It is a tremendous fight to heal and to reinvest in your life again. You are not the same person during, and even after the holes matte themselves back together.

If your holes come before you get your luxury, the luxury has to find those holes and probe until he understands and can offer comfort when you need to cry and laugh with you when you need to relive memories or be proud for you when you want to regale him with stories. If your luxury is entrenched in your life and a tidal wave hits, he has to ride the wave with you. It is as traumatic for them as for you. They are afraid of losing you because your behavior becomes erratic and unpredictable. They are just as lost and in as much pain as you.

My ultra-traumatic holes in my soul came much later. Long after I had met, married, and raised kids with my Studmuffin. Life was good. My parents were healthy, still traveling and having fun. My three sisters were happy and healthy, as were my two brothers. We girls and mom cruised every year with who ever wanted to tag along. My brothers were great, nearing retirement, traveling and enjoying their own families. The family was a huge organism in its own right. Nothing could take this family down to their knees...

One morning, my mom called me and told me to meet her at Dixie Café at noon and to ask no questions. I arrived to find my other two sisters that lived in town waiting, too. We sat there giggling, wondering where mom was taking us. Mom appeared very somber and asked for a table in the back. We were stricken because, by the look on her face, we knew something bad was about to happen. As she told us about our sister Sally's cancer, she handed me the biopsy reports. I am also a nurse and as I read them, I read a death sentence. Hole number one had just come from a cannon right through our hearts.

We started back to back forays to New Jersey to take care of our beloved sister. She lived nearly three months.

On the heels of Sally's death, Brother John was diagnosed. Hole number two. We lived chemo to chemo and scan to scan, and he went into remission beautifully for several years. Even in remission he took chemo and did scans. With each procedure, you tell yourself it's ok, but that hole just quivers like Jell-O, and you can't breathe a whole breath.

One morning, on a day we were expecting a bad scan result from John, I was awakened at 5 a.m. to the news that Keith's cousin had died. At 6 a.m. came the news that my sister Becky was at ER. Several tests and hours later a doctor walked into her ER room and said, "It's cancer of the colon with mets to the liver," and walked out. Fire in the hole; there is number three. After the surgery to clear the bowel blockage, we were told palliative care only, and we might have two years with chemo.

John came out of remission. He never made remission again.

One afternoon, Brother Drew made his weekly phone call to the parents and reported he had bronchitis. The bronchitis cleared, but the chest pain did not. X-rays revealed problems with his heart. Stents failed. Bypass failed too, and he died from complications of open heart surgery. One more cannon ball-sized hole.

We took Becky on one last cruise, and we made sure that she got to do anything she wanted. Upon return, she steadily declined, and we once again buried one of our parents' precious children.

John was the last. He died about a year after Becky.

That leaves two daughters, myself and Phyllis. Our parents, ages eighty-three and ninety- two dote on us and react with fear if we sneeze too loud. They make it a point to be close to the many many five generations' worth of children that they still have, but the holes in their souls have definitely taken a toll. We have a family cruise planned for June, and I admire them tremendously for being strong enough to take this epic adventure on. I am so thankful for the gift it is going to be for our family.

They have stood together through it all, bonded together like super glue. They have faced every second of every crisis intertwined. With them, it is difficult to see where one ends and the other begins. They have the ultimate luxury, even now with the many holes in their collective souls that I am convinced they are intertwined into one soul, they still stand together. You can frequently, especially in stressful days, find them cuddled together on Mom's couch. They can and have been hurt, but their bond is unbreakable, luxurious even in pain.

I tell you this extremely personal experience that lasted nine years to illustrate what serious holes can exist in our souls. Now to examine what they do to relationships. Can you guess? Holes in our souls affect our relationships. Man, is that an understatement.

As I stated earlier, Keith and I had been married over half our lives, our kids were grown and gone on their ways. We aren't only talking my family but his, too. They love him, and he has been integrated into the family for many, many, many years, and he was torn between his own pain and fear for me.

He knew very well how integrated and blended our family is. Although our parents stressed individuality, and we are definitely very diverse in personality and talent, we are all one tree with deep intertwined roots and many strong branches that all merge into one living organism that functions as one and as many. He had no clue how to approach comforting me and dealing with his own pain. Frankly, his attempts with Sally were ill-fated and later a bone of contention within our relationship. However, as things progressed, he accepted that it was happening and that it was tearing me in pieces and for the early times, all he could do was watch and try to hold me when I cried.

He was, however, scared of the anger, and I had a lot of anger. I grew up in a family that was so tight and so constantly tended that I thought life was fair, at least in our family. But suddenly, nothing was fair and there was no fairy tale ending in sight, and I demanded that. It was one big giant hole in my soul, and my luxury wanted so desperately to patch it.

A luxury can't fix us. Remember we have to fix ourselves and then add a luxury. So, for much of the time, he was standing there watching the woman he loves with his whole soul fall to pieces. His fear was massive. I was lost to me. He felt he was losing his luxury.

However, all said and done, minus two sisters and two brothers, I still have serious holes in my soul. My soul is still spinning mother of pearl and spattering paper machete over the holes filled with memories and love. My luxury is still here. When I came back to myself, he was right where I left him, in my arms and in my soul. There were times I wasn't even aware he was there. There were times I demanded more from him than he could give. There were times that my absent shell just laid in his arms and tried to will myself to come back to me, and me to him.

We put everything back into place and began having fun again and then one more tragedy struck. This time the hole shot through my Studmuffin's heart. His dad died. I had some relapse, but that was deflected by caretaking the man who fathered my luxury.

When he began hospice care, I slipped into my normal role in his family and became caregiver and comfort. Keith and I were there day and night, a team. We did it together. In perfect sync, our family flawlessly, with no regrets or no dissention worked together to escort our beloved Burnette patriarch out of this world and into the arms of his parents, his youngest son, and, of course, the arms of the Lord.

I have stood by Keith as he has assumed the patriarch role on this family with both pride and grief. I have done the best I could to be his luxury as he and I have healed and taken on new roles.

We gained another granddaughter through the transition as our only niece on his side decided she wanted to be our granddaughter like our granddaughter, Kaylee. We readily agreed. Our niece, Avery, has little family on her dad's side, and no one can have too many grandparents. You would think it would be hard being both aunt/uncle and Nene/Papa, but it has been seamless and feels good to say we have two granddaughters instead of just one.

I am busy building our granddaughters' libraries. Nene loves books and believes in reading at a young age. Papa always makes sure there are two-dollar bills in his overall pocket when the family gathers. Yes, the holes are still there, but a good luxury helps heal the pain and carries you when you can't put one foot in front of the other. I have a wonderful luxury.

When you see those special couples that emanate 'oneness,' you know they are two emotionally healthy individuals that have become each other's luxury. They complement each other, finish each other's sentences, and move in unison. They are one luxurious organism that lives both in autonomy and in complete unity. But make no mistake, there are holes in both their souls. They are each aware and intricately entrenched in each other's because they are part of the comfort and the cure.

The holes in our soles are personal, internal spaces that very few are granted the security level to know or to see. It takes a tremendous amount of trust to bare the holes in your soul. A healthy, near self-actualized person has healthy boundaries. Boundaries define relationships, and not all relationships are material for deep inner trust. It is a badge of honor and of obligation to be privy to an emotionally healthy person's holes in his or her soul. Only a smattering of people need apply. Some family, friends, and, of course, that luxury you bring into your life has to be made privy and to be allowed to react to those holes. That luxury needs to know when to hold you, when to talk you through an anniversary or any painful time, and also when to navigate around triggers to keep you from reopening that hole. That, my friends, is what you want to find in your luxury as it relates to holes in your soul.

To be able to achieve all the aforementioned goals with the holes, a number of characteristics must be present. Your luxury must be at about the same level of self-actualization as you. Your luxury must know you as well as he knows the back of his hand, to use an old adage. Your luxury must know where the holes are and the power of each to knock you to the ground and what is likely to trigger that. Your luxury must be willing to lend you a hand up and help dust you off. He must be empathetic and loving regarding these holes.

It must be noted that a mate who is not luxury material will use these holes as power. They will thrust a figurative sword into these holes without remorse. This is why a healthy person only reveals holes to certain trustworthy and loving people. Something you bought on clearance or without doing your research can actually inflict more misery than having bought nothing. At least you won't torture your own weak links. Someone, however, who is a user or an abuser will do it in a heartbeat because his goal is not in sync with yours. It is his alone. If you don't immediately comply with what he wants, he attacks the weakest part of your soul. He goes straight for those holes in your soul and utilizes the pain to gain compliance. He does not give you the hand up or the dusting off either.

Too many people live in relationships like this. They are with people who utilize pain and power to manipulate and break their partner's soul. They have no desire or intention of helping patch the holes; they want them open and bleeding for a reason. Too many children are being raised in these flawed relationships as well, and they grow up to find the same dysfunction and chaos within relationships. A cycle is begun and perpetuated in just two generations.

Make sure you are the first and find a luxury, not an old clunker with poor motives. Enjoy your lives together and watch the second generation do the same. Then move into your golden years and watch the majority of five generations do it like my parents have with love, adventure and respect

# Communication

Nena and I are great communicators; we have spent lifetimes in nursing, social work, professional counseling, and marriage and family therapy. We married good ole boys from rural Arkansas who speak an entirely different language.

I married a man who didn't just want to "rock the boat." He wanted and still wants a life without drama, is incredibly friendly, sweet, and a good guy. He is also an incredible flirt, hugs multiple women in Walmart, and could talk to a fence post. When we first got married, we would go into Walmart, and as I began to pull my hair out when I couldn't find him, I used a communication tool developed before the cell phone, the public address system. "Kerry Keasler to the service desk, your wife is looking for you." Sometimes you have to use whatever tool is available. There are lots of tools you can use to communicate effectively with your partner. Among them, for me, are the follows:

- Honesty, having an open relationship where you tell each other the truth is important, letting your partner know how you feel about what you like what you don't. Not being honest can lead to the discussion of "Why don't you ever wear the pants suit I got you for Christmas that you said you liked so well?" "Oh, you mean the one where I could hear people laughing in the court room whenever I wear it?" was not the honest response. I hurt his feelings. The honest response might have been, "I really don't like double knits, and that mint green isn't among my favorite colors, but let's go take it back together and find something we both like." Maybe honesty back then might have improved some less-than-perfect Christmas mornings.

- Listen, really listen, and recognize that listening is both with your ears but with your eyes as well. Look at body language. What your partner is saying by his or her actions?" Example: When your wife comes in and rips the broken blinds out of the wall, maybe taking them down six months ago when she asked might have been a good idea.

- Learn and practice fair fighting rules such as keeping things in the here and now, not throwing in the kitchen sick, no name-calling. Lift each other up even when you might be mad. Count to ten...or fifty, whatever it takes for you to get yourself under control. It is never okay to lay your hands on your partner in anger or violence, never okay to call them names, or your children or your partner's parents' names. Putting down your family in from of your partner or your kids will result in the children and your partner not respecting your family. Be willing to recognize that there will be things in every family, with each other, where you don't come to consensus. Revisit those things as needed. Just learn to deal with those that will never be resolved if you have your luxury and plan on keeping him/her.

- Spend time each day you have together in intimacy, and I'm not just talking about sex, but that certainly is an excellent way if both are true participants, not one just interested in getting off and not sharing intimacy with their partner. Intimacy might mean making your partners coffee or bringing them that Diet Coke. It may mean holding hands, at church, at the movies, in the middle of the night. My parents were wonderful hand holders. When my dad was weeks from death, Mother decided to have us turn in their beds we had pushed together so they could better hold hands with their heads facing each other's feet. They were doing such when she called me to the room to tell me "Daddy's gone." Intimacy is telling each other on the phone, or when we are walking out the door, "I love you." We tell our grown children we love them often. Even times when we may not like their behavior, we love them.

- Communication means talking...really talking. It means talking about the hard stuff, our sorrows and embarrassments, our failures. It's telling our partner when they have hurt us but willing to listen when they tell us we have hurt them. It is not letting things fester and come to a head, for a gross example. I suggest taking time as you lie in bed to discuss your day to share happiness or sorrow, something fun you did or a conversation you have had with a friend or grandchild. But if you have a husband whose head hits the pillow and he's out, you need to find another time. I am not a morning person, but since retirement, and a couple of shoulder surgeries, I have been getting up with my husband, the school bus driver, at 5:00 am and having coffee, talking about school and his family, my family, our kids, the grands and how much trouble the granddaughters are on his bus. Ha. We are struggling with the death of my parents and his father; we daily deal with his mother's Alzheimer's and watching her personality and her ability to function disappear before our eyes. We deal with problems between our children, between other relatives, financial difficulties, health issues, and adjustment to retirement, which are struggles that many couples deal with. I cannot magically make those issues disappear, but I can communicate with my luxury. Together we can face anything.

When we were first married, I used the now unheard skill of letter writing. When I would try to talk to him (usually about how the kids were driving me nuts or how angry I was because whatever issue), I felt we needed to address what he was avoiding talking about, an issue that had come up while he was away on guard drill, and I couldn't wait until he had taken a bath in bleach to kill the chiggers. I would write pages and pages and then leave them in the robe of his pocket, taped to the mirror, or the steering wheel of his car. He would read it, and I would have calmed down by then, and the chiggers didn't itch as much. We would talk, and often I would cry. I hate that I cry when angry, stressed, or hurt. He has been wonderful at not seeing tears as emotional blackmail because it isn't, or at least, my tears are not intended to be. Sometimes my words turn to liquid before I can get them out.

# Power

Power is a big word and an even bigger concept. How power is used and divided in a relationship is very important. Many believe that in all societies and cultures, the man has ultimate power. This simply is not true. There are many matriarchal societies and cultures throughout history and even today.

There is external power and internal power. Every soul has some amount of both.

Internal power is our point of control. It feeds our sense of self. It feeds our sense of security and belongingness. It tells us who we are, and it provides individuality. When we look at a potential mate, we must take into account that internal power and if this is the one, we must accept their internal sense of power. This is not something you should go into looking to change because it is part of our core personality. If you cannot accept someone's locus of control, then you should throw them back into the pond. We must not break people. In addition, if a basic part of their personality is wrong for you, the whole person, valuable as they are, is wrong for you.

Our internal power projects our strengths and protects our weaknesses. It's like the big sister of the personality. It may be healthy, it may not be, but still it is a basic part of who we are, and we are the only ones who can change that. We have to want to change it, and not because someone wants to change it.

Now that we have looked at internal power, let's look at power in a relationship. Who should have power over what? There are certainly some preconceived beliefs within our cultures over who should have power and who should not. Pish posh, whatever works is the answer, and if no one is being exploited or hurt, it is no one's business.

It also is not set in stone. As a relationship grows and changes, power distribution often changes as well. As a newly married couple, and for about the first fifteen years, I had the power (chore) of taking care of the money. My husband was an over the road truck driver, and it just made sense for me to keep up with the bills and money (or lack thereof at times).

Now, I am so happy to say that I have no clue what is in the bank, what is paid, and what is due. I tell him when I feel a shopping trip coming on, he hands me money, if we can afford it at that time. I don't question anything, unless I come home and there is no electricity. Then it's kind of like an open season on advanced age maladies rather than a fight. It doesn't matter who or if both do the money as long as things get done and no one is slighted or placed in an inferior role over who has the power of money.

Power comes into play in many ways within a relationship. Power to display and act with individuality is also dependent on power. Power used unwisely can squash independence and individuality. We must be careful not to become power hungry and try to squash these traits of our spouse because of our own insecurities or hunger for control. We chose this person partially because of these traits. It makes no sense, unless trust has been broken, to tamper with them now.

As I sit her typing, my husband is out with his lifelong best friend. Their original destination was the race track to watch our friend's son race a motorcycle. I am sure that that was the primary destination. However, there is no curfew in our relationship. They may end up anywhere, and I am sure that I have nothing to worry about, so why would I object?

A few weeks ago, my friends and I did the time warp. We left the house in strange clothes, to say the least, late at night and came in even later at night…or it could have been early the next morning. Our husbands just laughed and joked about resurrecting the *Rocky Horror* experience at our age. Again, the trust hasn't been broken, so no worries, no power struggles. We went, threw toast, toilet paper, and various other things. We yelled at the screen and sang with the songs. We had a great girl's night out.

We did not return home to angry husbands, just husbands who have trouble sleeping well without us. No backlash, just as there will be no back lash whenever hubby wanders in today or tonight. Our power is shared and largely dormant because no trust has been broken. Power changes after trust is broken. It becomes more out in the open and plays a large role in regaining trust. If a relationship is to remain in place after broken trust, the partner will not be so lenient with power for the person who broke trust.

For a time, power will be in the hands of the innocent and the breaker of trust must win back TRUST in order to regain power and send power back to dormancy. Personal power, to be a free ranging chick or rooster, very much depends on trust and responsibility. If one breaks the rules, the trust and power has to be re-earned. So, must the love be rebuilt.

However, if both choose to stay, once trust is reasonably re-earned, it must be tested and re-given. It is unfair to hold ultimate power forever. Holding total power breeds resentment and dissention in the ranks. It will take a relationship down like the Hindenburg.

No one person should have all the power in a relationship. Totalitarianism ruins most relationships. At the very least, the relationship will be unstable, and the one with no power will always be nervous and afraid. Suffice it to say, this is not healthy.

Power should be negotiated from the beginning. If you find a potential mate and all the dates go his way with no deference to what you might want or think, Run. You have a control freak.

Many people who have not done the self-work or been brought up successfully within the Maslow or similar model think that a control freak is a good thing. They see someone to take care of all the things they are unsure about. They see the typical princess being rescued by the prince on the white horse. What they are really getting is life in prison. They will never have any power, and everyone needs to have personal power. Controlling people are major red flag material. Run; run away.

It is much healthier to do the self- work on your own, find out who you are and where your internal power lies. Learn to be you. Learn to take care of you. If you do this and become a healthy inner and outer person, then meet a control freak...you will automatically cast them out of your kingdom. Likewise, they will not be interested in you in the least...hell, you might want to go out and do the Time Warp at midnight, and that would not be allowed in their kingdom.

What you will look for is a person who wants to share power. Sometimes they want to eat Mexican and just have a strong craving, and you will most likely give in because you know that next time you will be in charge. You may want to do the Time Warp, and he may want to go to the races independent of each other... so what? You end up together at the end of the day with two separate adventures to share and laugh about.

Then there are times that it doesn't matter what you do, as long as you are together holding hands and laughing together. It is shared power that works itself out because your relationship is well-oiled, and the engine is running smoothly.

Power over the big stuff is a little more complex. The big stuff, where you live, children, how to raise them, and religion are just a few examples of the big stuff. Negotiating the big stuff successfully requires two emotionally healthy people debating, sharing thoughts both large and small about each big thing. It is not something over which either can have total power. These things are often deal breakers that can easily end a relationship, or at the very least, make it very unhappy.

Each big thing must be debated and earnestly discussed from every angle with respect for self and other. They are serious subjects that determine a direction of one part of your relationship for the long haul, and most are set in motion and not derailed once the decision has been made and set free to thrive.

Where to live can be a big one. This one may be dictated by how close to which family to live. Sounds like a simple one, but it assuredly is not. Each of you were raised in a completely different environment, and it can be a real struggle fitting into your chosen one's family if you choose to live near them.

Husband and I made that mistake and moved almost immediately to 'the hill' on which his family lived. It was, at that time, a mistake of mammoth proportions. It nearly cost us our marriage. We had to move away, and he who had never imagined living anywhere else, made that sacrifice for our marriage to move away. Years later, the kids are grown, and the two of us are more mature, so we moved back to the hill. It wasn't peaches and cream still, and finally there was a big blow up and now, thankfully, we are all on even ground and a happy family on the hill. I will spend the rest of my days with my husband on this hill. And I am at peace with that. I am at home.

Not everyone has a smooth transition. We certainly didn't. Power of the in-laws. Seems like a strange place to find power, does it not?

Trust me, it is there. We normally go into a relationship expecting the same environment in our relationship as in our family of origin. In addition, our family of origin may apply pressure to make that happen. Now think seriously about this scenario. We have two people from two completely different families of origin, two mini cultures that are entrenched in both parties in the relationship.

Soon, the two of you will hit a wall somewhere embedded in one of those mini cultures. It could be over dating practices, religion, children, communication...and the list goes on and on.

My family is very laid back, accepting, and loud. We speak our mind then talk things through. Often it comes down to agreeing to disagree, and that is what we do. We travel in packs. We love each and every person that enters our family. And much of our family is inherited, but they are just as important as those born to us. We talk loud and uncensored. We laugh loud and uncensored. We are who we are, and what you see is what you get.

My husband's family is more conventional and communicates differently than mine. He was raised in a more traditional multi-generational family setting. They, all lived and loved on their hill. Much like the Waltons. Finding my niche is this family dynamic was quite difficult at times. Happily, I can now say that I feel at home and am respected and belong on this crazy beautiful hill with our family.

Negotiation is the key. Sit down, roll your sleeves up, pour a glass of wine (just don't tell his family, stop by my parents' and dad will give you a bottle), and start talking. Explain, in detail, how your family works, including who has the power because that isn't always obvious. If the kids have the power...run...they aren't good at governing the family.

Talk about traditions. Talk about child rearing. Talk about roles. Talk about strengths and who has which strengths. Talk about who is the go-to person for what problems. Talk about your childhood within your family. Definitely talk about any and all quirkiness!

As you share these pieces of yourself and your family, you are growing as a couple, and you are building your own version of what your own family will be. In the best-case scenario, you will adopt a little of both sides and will fall somewhere in the middle with a stable family system with a little quirkiness for fun's sake.

This method also tends to build a solid balance of power within the relationship. It's a beautiful side effect of sharing and communication of what is important to each of you. During this process, you see where power is important to each of you, and you, by default, give and take. You give power that is important to one and take power that is important to you. Family interference will happen. How you manage it is important. Again, go back to negotiation stages and decide how important the family member's transgression is and decide what action or communication is needed.

Always stand up for your mate, unless they were the transgressor and were in the wrong. Many families will pick at a new family member if allowed to do so. Once they see that no matter what they do to the person, it's on like donkey kong, and they will make that person's life miserable. It's hard to fight back when your spouse isn't standing behind you.

In the same vein, it's hard for a family to fight back if your child will not stand up for you. Once a new entry takes a pot shot and it is tolerated…same precedent is set …it's on. The family can't fight back because of fear of losing their child and /or grandchildren. Yes, some parents withhold grandchildren simply because they can get away with it. They like the power. This power should be smashed by the other parent. Respect for your family of origin is important. Each side of the family has traditions and culture to teach their younglings. Children need as many grandparents as possible to love and support them.

Religion is a big one as well. When you engage in a relationship that is an interfaith relationship, this should be addressed, especially if the relationship is more than a dalliance. Once again roll your sleeves up, pour a glass of wine if your faith allows, and discuss to the bottom of your soul what your faith means to you and how important it is to you. This will probably take more than one discussion, and it is personal. Do not allow in-laws or extended family members be a part of this. It is between the two of you. Ultimately, you may have children and how you are going to worship should be already decided.

Many couples worship both denominations in some system of cooperation and sharing. When children are of age to decide, they are allowed to choose. Some people declare this a deal breaker, and the other concedes power. I pray that the one conceding power is doing so because it matters less to her than to her significant other. Just conceding to avoid a fight can plant a seed of dissention that may erupt nastily at any time, especially when children enter the picture.

Careers can turn into a power struggle too. My husband respects what I do, but he is not terribly fond of the idea. I love working with the chronically mentally ill, and it worries him. He realizes that I understand what I am doing and that he has just a vague idea and some tv references and what others have told him. When I declared my last major, he certainly wasn't happy. Neither was my daddy, for that matter. But both respected me and had enough faith in me to refrain from pulling rank and forbidding me from chasing my dream.

When a career requires moving, such as military, both must be on board. I applaud those who make it work. It is something that I don't think I could ever be on board with. For many, repeated moves are deal breakers. For others, repeated moves are just one more adventure. Respect people for who they are and pray they find someone with similar adventures in mind. Thank God every night for those families in the military who protect our wonderful country.

And for us homebodies that value family interconnectedness over moving around, thank God every night for those police officers that make our neighborhoods safe.

Remember when negotiating moving around, negotiate power and veto power because the time may come when one just can't make one more move. Respect that. People change, and what used to be just another adventure may turn into a deep-seated dread or fear. Respect it, work through it, and don't just pull rank.

Sex. Do not ever use sex as power. Using sex as power sets an intolerable precedent. It takes away trust. It takes away intimacy. It takes away independence and autonomy. It takes away power from the other party. It takes away the privilege of sharing your body, your soul, and your love for that person. It is a gift to be given and received with respect and love.

Some have agreed up on roles and rules about sex. As long as both agree on those rules, roles, techniques, and have a safe word, then it becomes a choice, not a power play. Everybody plays, but not everybody plays the same way. As long as no one is being taken for granted or advantage of, then play on.

If at any time one wants to change the rules, shake things up, try something new, negotiate, share feelings honestly, and if you are both on the same page, go ahead. However, both have veto power to exercise at any time.

# Sex

There cannot be a book about relationships without including a chapter on sex, so here it is. All relationships include sexuality in one way or another. By nature, we are all sexual creatures. By nature, we all have our natural desires and drives that may or may not be compatible with others. Being ashamed of sexuality is a crying shame. Being responsible for your sexuality is a must. Understanding and being comfortable in your sexuality is a plus and hopefully a must. Understanding that there are many types and styles of sex is also a must. Experimenting is also a must, so don't have a meltdown when you realize that your kids or even you yourself hit one of those experimental stages. There is more than one experimental stage.

Those points being made, let's move forward. The Experimental stage of sex, is both the first and the last type of sex. Yes, you read that right. Initially, children grow to adolescence and begin to experiment. We all remember that first kiss, that first cuddle, that classic categorization of "the bases." We remember that initially it was in the back of our minds and then suddenly, BAM, it is front and center!

For me it was seeing that tanned boy swimming across the pool with his black curls floating behind him. My brain never thought about what sexuality was in the same way again. I'm not saying, of course, that I wanted to throw down and have full out sex on the side of the pool, but a touchy-feely hug was definitely forefront in my mind. Is that first base? I never quite understood the base system.

I remember taking my children and one of my son's friends to a local circus. Somewhere during the show, a young woman appropriately clad as an acrobat entered the show. I smiled as I saw my son's friend break out in a sweat, turn beet red, and appear to have some difficulty catching his breath. BAM! He had been struck down, his sexuality just hit him in the heart like a sledge hammer. It happens to us all at some point. It is a rite of passage of the human experience.

Once we move through this rite of passage, true experimentation begins. We begin to interact with the opposite sex in a different way (if that is our orientation). We see everyone as potential, but we don't know what to do and how to do it. Thus, we spend a few years practicing. We daydream, we kiss mirrors, and we dance to music and pretend the special crush of the week is holding us tight. It is a time filled with angst and questions, day dreams, and for boys anyway, some special night time dreams.

Our bodies and our emotions are maturing. Our communication is maturing too. We begin to communicate a little more efficiently, and eventually, that first dance, that first kiss, that first clumsy make out session in a dark corner and so on, all the way to our first 'time' happens.

This is all natural and normal. Timing is according to moral teachings and personal beliefs and for reality…throw in a little impulsivity. I refuse to enter the argument of sex before or after marriage. If a child is brought up with proper body knowledge, personal religious beliefs, and close family open to communication, that young person will make the best choice for themselves.

On the other hand, I must unfortunately state that many kids aren't brought up in healthy environments. They may be neglected or abused physically or sexually. They also may be taught that sexuality is shameful. These young adults seldom have innate healthy sexuality and frequently make unhealthy choices. They have to do the self-work to transform themselves into healthy individuals looking for a luxury, but that is another chapter all together.

As we move toward our adult selves, our sexuality likewise matures. We begin to look for possible mates, and sexuality takes its place in our adult brain, heart, and body. We react to that part of ourselves according to our belief system, again, throw in a little impulsivity.

We date, or whatever it is called today. We practice. Through trial and error, we decide what we like and do not like. Again, how far we go around the bases is a decision for each person. We all have our personal boundaries. Shame is a word that needs to be far removed from sex. Even sex one is pressured or forced into should not result in the victim feeling shame…the responsibility and the shame for that is on the perpetrator.

Sex for love is a beautiful event. It is a natural event. It is an instinctual act. It is the first type of sex that I want to talk about.

When you find someone that you feel love and attachment to, when you have experimented with petting and foreplay. and that just doesn't seem enough any longer, your metaphorical heart makes the decision that it is time to move to the final level and let it all ride.

It is not an act of shame. It is an act of intimacy, of giving yourself completely to someone that you love and trust. It is beautiful. It is natural. It is all encompassing in your heart and soul. When two bodies meet, connect, and share all…elation is the word that comes to mind. This type of sex more than connects two bodies, it connects two souls.

If this relationship continues to mature and is or becomes a marriage or long-term relationship, this is the ultimate experience that you learn to create over and over. You learn to love and revere both your own body and your partner's body for what they do and for each other. Hopefully this is the type of sex you most frequently go to because it creates a channel of bond and communication that cannot exist elsewhere. It is a necessity for long term relationships. It requires respect, love, honesty, openness, and reverence.

Make up sex. Many love make up sex. I understand many people fight so they can engage in makeup sex. Ok. No, I don't understand the concept because I hate to fight. However, just because I do not understand it, it does not make it at all invalid. I hear many juicy, hot stories about makeup sex. Bottom line, as long as it is consensual and respectful of boundaries…. live it up, Buttercup!

Recreational sex is another type of sex. I think everyone who is sexually active engages in recreational sex. Single people may use recreational sex just to meet a biological need, or in layman's terms… to scratch an itch. If you have a healthy sexuality and are at peace with this, then continue on, but I still am pulling for you to one day find the intimate lovemaking sex as well.

People in long term relationships also engage in recreational sex. It's playful and tension releasing. It puts a fun spin on relationships. Some even role plays and pretend it's a one-night stand or a tryst. They do it to keep things spiced up. They do it to revisit youth when adulthood gets too heavy. They do it just for fun. It is perfectly healthy. They also do it to, here is that word again…experiment. Try new things, fantasize, or test out new techniques. Just be sure to have a safe word in case things get uncomfortable for either party. Have fun. As long as you are consenting, respectful adults, it's all good. No shame, sex is healthy.

Another type of sex, maybe a variation on recreational sex, is sex for exercise. You have to admit, it burns a lot of calories, and it tones muscles. If you don't feel like running a mile in the rain…work out with your partner. This type of sex is fun and spontaneous…have fun with it. Afterwards, eat a decadent meal. After all, you've already worked it off.

Sex, fortunately, does not end. It adapts. To adapt, one must experiment. Injuries happen, babies happen, body degeneration due to age happens. I remember one of my professors, while talking on the subject of sex making the statement …what I used to could do all night, now it takes me all night to do.

Sex is important in relationships, and it may change, but it needs to remain an important part of every relationship. Even if one can no longer achieve traditional intercourse, adapt, remain sexual with your partner.

However, intercourse can almost always be achieved. It takes resolve, willingness to experiment, and patience. We all get older, get injured, and have illnesses or physical decline. If you still love that person beside you, adapt. Experiment. Find a way to continue to please each other sexually.

If intercourse cannot be achieved, then use other methods of sexuality. It may be that you end up holding each other naked, stroking each other, and reminiscing. This will reconfirm the intimate side of your love and please your bodies as well. Sexuality never dies, so never deny it or stop soothing it. Again, sexuality is healthy, so never be ashamed. If it becomes impossible, continue to hold hands, rub backs, nibble on necks, kiss deeply and hug long and tight every chance you get.

# Break Ups

(**Nena**) Even in the best of circumstances, breakups happen. Breakups happen for a number of reasons. They are unfortunately, and sometimes fortunately, an important part of life.

As we grow old enough to begin to be interested in sexuality, we begin to "go out," "go steady," "date," or dream of participating in these activities and whatever other adjectives for relationships are going around in this day and time. We dream, we observe or leer, as the case may be. We begin to tentatively identify people to whom we are attracted. First, we fantasize about that first kiss, that first date, all the firsts that go along with exploring couple-hood, relationships, and sexuality. It is a heady, dreamy time in our lives. I am sure we all have a smile on our face when we recall those thoughts, dreams, and events. Then most likely a chuckle when we consider what would have happened if those first forays into true love would have stuck. Thank God for the prayers unanswered, huh? However, those forays were valuable and were, let's face it, fun.

I still grin from ear to ear when I remember the summer before we started 7th grade. One of my sister's friends had rented Reynolds swimming pool for a night party. I can still vividly see those brown shoulders and arms; topped by the blackest curly hair I had ever seen swimming across the water. I can still feel the excitement, too. I tried so hard to get that boy to notice me and failed. I still remember the disappointment, too, because he never did.

I found out at the beginning of school in 7th grade when all the grade schools combined that that beautifully tanned boy.... was blind as a bat. I could have danced naked by the pool and he would never have noticed because most people do not swim with their glasses on. Eventually, he did notice. I have some wonderful memories from that relationship, and I know he does too. That was a love that was

71

hard to die and that I grieved relentlessly for a long, long time, but again, Thank God for unanswered prayers. I am sure in retrospect, he would agree.

Recently, he and I had our chance to talk. We reminisced and answered each other's questions. We smiled, laughed, and said goodbye one last time. I learned a lot from that relationship, gained much insight. I took away many snippets of treasured feelings that I still hold in my heart. It was an adventure. It was a learning experience.

Then there was the one that my momma was convinced I would marry and never part from. While she loved him dearly, she did see the "bad boy" and worried for me, not about me, but for the type of life she could envision I would have with him. She knew it was not the life I wanted, as much as I truly loved him. I had better insight than she realized. Even though I loved that boy with my heart and soul, I too, knew our worlds, our goals, our values were too different. We tried again and again, but it never worked out. Every time he came back around, I heard the words to Dolly Parton's song, "Here You Come Again" spinning around in my head as my heart rate raced. Eventually we came to terms that it never would work itself into a long-term relationship, as much as we both wanted it to. That was probably my first "mature" love. It was deeply rooted in my soul, just as the memories still are.

If I ran into him today I am sure we would spend hours catching up and would still feel a connection and comfort with each other that we had from the day we met. But love, in the lasting sense, was never meant to be for us. I hope he is a happy family man somewhere. I pray he found a luxury that settled in his heart and stayed; he deserves it.

I also made the 'date a friend' mistake. That is a harsh judgment, though, because the only thing I regret about that relationship was that we both hurt someone we each treasured. Our love for each other was real and precious, but in a friendship mode, so it of course burned out. The love did not; the boyfriend/girlfriend dynamic took a nasty fall. He was a wonderful young man. He died in a tragic accident at a young age. I would love to have had one last hug. I wish his family love and countless peak experiences of the memories of who he was.

I share these parts of my life to demonstrate the dynamic I am about to describe. We practice. We grow and mature and practice at developing relationships. We practice recognition of people we are attracted to or compatible with. It is, perhaps, a bad analogy but it is like trying on shoes; we search for the one kind that fits, supports, and is pleasing to the eyes.

That is what dating is about, from the earliest crush to the ultimate commitment to our luxury. We practice. We fine tune who we are and how we relate to people. Through these practice games, or even battle exercises in some cases, we are learning about ourselves, learning about people, and learning about life. We are moving toward adulthood and toward self-actualization. Because we are perfecting our self-actualizing traits, methodology, and also because the people we practice with are doing the same, growing, maturing, self-actualizing; breakups are inevitable in our early years.

Breakups are heart-wrenching. We grieve, and we are sure that the world is not going to make another revolution because it simply cannot survive the amount of pain we are projecting into the atmosphere! Do not laugh. In our early years we are that dramatic. Embarrassing, is it not? Who among us cannot picture the episode of *King of the Hill* where Bobby lies face down in a pool of tears listening to "Tear in My Beer" over and over again?

Sadly, but also thankfully, we have all had that or a similar experience. It is all part of growing up and finding out who we are and who we want to be a luxury, not a necessity. In a way, these early relationships are a necessity, or at the very least, a rite of passage. They teach us to better identify ourselves and who is a viable, optimistic choice. They teach us to look for attributes and traits that complement ourselves rather than recklessly falling madly in love with the tan shoulders and black curly locks swimming across a pool. They teach us that mature love really has nothing about superficial traits or hapless availability. Long term luxury has nothing to do with the tall, broad shouldered, tiny-waisted guy that keeps waltzing back into our life and the excitement he emanates.

The point of these early forays into love is to learn by process of elimination, trial and error. That was fun while it lasted but after your broken heart mends, you learn that it did not last for a reason and can identify what that reason was. This knowledge is utilized to further define self and stored for future comparison when we are about to repeat that fun, but inappropriate, type of relationship.

This is, of course, in direct opposition to earlier generations, pre-industrialization when these first relationships would most likely become permanent. Then it would more likely have been long lasting because of the fact that there were few choices. Most likely, you would have been nurtured in much the same way. Career and education paths would have been much the same. Family beliefs and religion would have been much the same, just because they were geographically connected. In this era, those first romances did often produce long term marriages.

This was because, in essence, from the point of meeting at a dating age, not much was going to change. Of course, it is also important to recognize that many relationships may not have started with romance as we see it now. Relationships were often arranged or at least encouraged by families and the church. Often friendships may have developed due to proximity and frequency of contact. They may be 'down the road a piece" from each other and attending social events centered around school and church.

In today's world however, through transition and adaptation, first loves are practice for later when we have discovered who we really are and where we are headed. We are learning numerous, things and practicing to perfect numerous skills.

As we begin to develop social skills, we begin to enter relationships. Hopefully we enter them with the knowledge that they are not meant to be permanent. They are a prelude to the real thing. The necessities are being met. By this, I mean that if we are emotionally healthy around puberty, having moved appropriately up through the hierarchy to this point, we begin to move from within our inner circle of family to investment in friendships. When friendships are, in turn, successful and we identify types of friends, we are able to honestly communicate and participate in a friendship. Feeding and nurturing friendships, in turn, gives us confidence and desire to develop more relationships. Then we begin to venture into romantic relationships. Each area of relationships that we have been a part of heretofore offers a sense of trust and belonging, and we healthfully venture forward.

We begin to experiment, to practice. Through this practice, we learn about others, about different types of relationships, and about ourselves. Interaction with others leads to self-search, further deepening our self-understanding and identity. Self-knowledge. Self-actualization.

These early breakups, though painful, hopefully serve their purpose. We are supposed to learn from our mistakes, not repeat them over and over. The early mistakes, breakups, should be analyzed and used as a spring board for the next relationship. By analyze, I mean explore what was right, what was wrong, what brought us joy, what brought us pain. In short, we are learning to identify the type of person who would be a luxury to the person we have become.

This is often where things go awry. Women I meet often jump in every relationship with both feet, without holding their breath or mapping the route. They choose the same type of person over and over. They never do the self-work to identify what works and what does not.

If the first relationship is abusive, they think maybe its normal, maybe they contributed to it; maybe they can fix the next one. Many factors fall into play here. But basically, once a certain type of person and relationship is chosen more than twice, a cycle is in place and recapitulates itself over and over. It makes no more sense than repeatedly touching the same hot stove. If people assume that relationships are supposed to be painful and necessary, they passively accept the cycle and have tremendous difficulty breaking it. They soon lose self-esteem and self-worth and quit trying to identify and know themselves and start making choices by default, not informed intelligent decisions. Unfortunately, they also usually procreate and model the cycle for their children to learn.

If you fall into this cycle or were born into this cycle, take heart. Anything that can be learned can also be unlearned. Cycles can be abandoned and broken and new behaviors learned. Do the self-work, the inner child work. Learn who you are and get comfortable with whom you are. If you find faults or weaknesses that you want to change, accept them, learn all about them, and change them to what you want them to be. Humans are very malleable and resilient creatures.

While it is true that our environment does shape us and control us as a child, once we become adults, we can take control and make our lives anything we want. Self-exploration does not start with a perfect person. Actually, there is no such thing. Self-exploration starts with identifying the self with acceptance, identifying and maximizing the strengths, then minimizing the weaknesses. Early break ups can help us do this on a whole other plane of existences; in fact, they fuel this process.

Through our early relationships, both romantic and platonic, we further define ourselves by how we fit into relationships with others and through seeing ourselves through the eyes of others.

As we approach adulthood, we should have a good insight into self and be comfortable with the self that we are. We are productive, self-efficient people capable of living our life in a healthy, productive way on our own. We move through the days in self-contentment, building our day to day existence. We become content, comfortable in our own skin. Our needs are met.

At this time, people begin to identify and seek their luxury. It is an adventure that would be a crime to avoid. Never miss a chance for an adventure. Begin shopping, but shop well, My Friends. Find a true luxury, whatever constitutes luxury for you. Once you find your luxury, continue to work to perfect your luxurious relationships. I sincerely hope that at this point you are one who never has to experience breakups again.

Unfortunately, even the best of relationships do hit snags and, for and indefinable number of reasons, wither and die. It is a sad fact of life. The ending of relationships, however, should not be seen as the end of the world. The relationship may end, but there are still two very distinct individuals who still are valuable, God-created creatures. Each half of these couples must move on and continue to be contributing members of society.

There is a healthy and an unhealthy way to break up. Remember that anger is a secondary feeling. It never stands alone. Anger is not even the primary emotion; it's the shield for the primary emotion. Anger is frequently at the forefront of a breakup. Usually it is hiding pain and/or grief.

Expressing anger is healthy. However, expressing anger needs to be respectful. Even though this person is no longer your significant other, they are still a valuable person on earth. You may even share children with this person. Children are a permanent tie and walking completely out of the other person's life is not plausible if you share children. They deserve, at the very least, basic human respect.

So, express away. It guides you to the process of grief. Anger is a part of grief, but it is only a part, not the entire thing. No matter what the reason for the breakup, a bond was forged. There are bound to be memories, shared adventures that will always be a part of who you are. To maintain the anger is to avoid the process of moving on, the process of growth. Growth is moving through the grief, yes, I said grief. No matter what the reason for the breakup, thankfulness for the adventure, for the shared feelings, and the growth while in the relationship all deserve recognition and processing to bring us toward healing.

We reinvest in ourselves and return back to being a self-actualizing individual. Just as after the death of a loved one, we grieve. Then we re-invest in life. The painful memories become beloved memories that, in time, come back to us in the form of peak experiences.

This is the healthy way to break up. Just simply decree no harm no foul and move on. Even if you were betrayed, grieving and letting go of the hurt allows you to return to emotional health and well-being. Not letting go of anger breeds and maintains more anger, maladaptive behaviors, and irrational thought patterns. This, in turn, leads to maladaptive behaviors and investing hastily in choices by default because vision is clouded by anger. Thought processes that are guided by rage and anger do not lead us toward healthy choices. In fact, quite the opposite, they lead us to further decline and further dysfunction.

It is important to forgive, reinvest in self, and move on. Remember that as an individual you entered these relationships to find a luxury, not because it was necessary that you find a mate.

Sometimes as humans we make mistakes and hurt the ones we love. Sometimes as individuals within a couple, we grow apart. Sometimes we flat screw up. If it cannot be repaired or if a deal breaker has occurred, review your relationship. Express your feelings of anger and grief. Allow yourself to grieve. Identify and treasure the memories, the milestones, and move on.

This type of breakup is emotionally healthy and, although you will grieve, you will also exit out the other side a wiser, more emotionally healthier person. For this, be thankful, and move on. Breathe in, breathe out, and move on.

# Peak Experiences

Peak Experiences. Peak experiences are transient moments of self-actualization. We are more whole, more integrated, more aware of ourselves and of the world during peak moments. At such times we think, act, and feel most clearly and accurately. We are more loving and accepting of others, have less inner conflict and anxiety, and are better able to put our energies to constructive use. Some people enjoy more peak experiences than others, particularly those Maslow called transcending self-actualizers

To be a self-actualizing person is to be at peace with self and have the knowledge and acceptance that we are always chasing self-actualization. It is an adventure of immense joy. Each day that we live and breathe, we change and hopefully grow in some way. We learn. We feel. We love. We work. We play. We develop beliefs, values, and goals. We internalize goals and move forward. We celebrate successes and the positives in our lives. We grieve failures and internalize what we learn from those failures. We accept responsibility for ourselves and for our actions and for our role in each relationship that we are involved in. We have no right to take responsibility and credit for our accomplishments if we do not likewise take responsibility of our mistakes. These things, in essence, are life.

We are not promised endless entertainment within a life of ease with no responsibilities. How would that be interesting? Life is not easy. More often than not, each day holds some struggles, disappointment, and pain. It is just the way things are. We exist in reality. As I type this, the analogy takes shape for me in the form of an old song, "I Never Promised You a Rose Garden" by Lynn Anderson.

A self-actualizing person accepts the challenge of life. Life is a journey. While it is true that there are trials and imperfections in every day, this is only part of the equation. There are also moments of intense joy. There are moments of intense love. There are moments of epiphany. This, too, is life. These are moments of peak experiences. They bring us joy. They bring us deep sense of peace and awe. They maintain hope and faith that life is worth the journey, that we have a purpose on this earth.

We do grow through overcoming adversity, which makes us stronger. We also grow and evolve through peak experiences. Peak experiences are intense moments of sheer pleasure, happiness. Peak experiences are moments of peace and well-being. Peak experiences are moments of belonging, a oneness with the world. Peak experiences are a sense of oneness with those we love. Peak experiences are a connection with spirituality.

In meditation, one achieves a transcendence of belonging, experiencing the unity of self with her higher power. In prayer, we also achieve this, a unity of self with God. My personal belief is that where God said we are created in his image, this unity is what is meant. That spirit, that soul is connected to, is an intertwined extension of God. In meditation and/or prayer, we achieve peak experiences, that oneness, that sense of peace and belonging. This type of peak experience gives our sole purpose and peace.

We as self-actualizing people also have, if we are open to them, peak experiences in every layer of our lives. This is why positive energy and thinking positive is so important. If we are focused on the negative, we often do not recognize or we refuse to acknowledge the peak experiences when they happen. It is very hard to recognize something so positive when we are deeply rooted in the negativity of every layer of our lives.

Self-actualizing persons will recognize, pause, and give themselves over to every peak experience they are given. When the moment passes, an emotionally healthy person will carefully store this moment and the feelings it produces deep within their heart and brain. They will thank God, or at least feel grateful to whatever they believe in as a higher power.

In the area of everyday life, I have innumerable peak experiences stored in my heart. I can pull up and re-experience each one at any time. They all strengthen my soul. They give me peace. They make me…me. I have already mentioned several peak experiences that have graced my life previously in earlier chapters. I will now add to those.

I spent many years at my grandma's heels, tending to flowers. I know the names of flowers and facts about flowers. Yet, I do not remember ever being taught this information. The knowledge of and love for flowers flowed seamlessly from grandma to me. Some years after she had died, my daughter and I were doing her annual birthday shopping excursion. I was solely focused on my child. I had no plans to buy anything for myself; this day was not about me. We were in a very crowded store when I walked up on two large beautifully framed paintings of irises, purple and orange. I was instantly mesmerized. Standing there looking at those pictures, I could feel her love wrapping itself around me just as it did when I was a young girl at her feet.

I bought the pictures. I cannot even imagine living somewhere without those two pictures. They are not great artwork. They were not expensive, but they speak to me. Thus, they are precious.

My mother is a very vibrant, larger-than-life person. She is outgoing, mischievous, and sometimes borderline mean, but in a harmless kind of way. Every day I am so thankful that she has so much fun and that she is always up for an adventure. The most meaningful, bonding moments I remember with her most all happened in the mornings.

My dad was always an early riser. Once he got up and started his day, I would leave my bed and go get in bed with Mom. We would lie there under the covers and talk. I would tell her all about what was going on in my life. We laughed and cried and planned. It seems so simple, but it was magical. It was our time.

I obviously have not lived with my parents for years. I probably miss those mornings with mom most of all. However, things change; we grow and transition on to independence.

Now, Mom keeps us all together as a family by her interactions in all of our fast-paced lives. She organizes big family cruises and is command central for all the travel 'preparations.' By preparations, I mean, of course, the matching cruise shirts, flip flops, bracelets, cruise purses, fun card holders, and of course the ever-popular cruise hats! These activities boost morale; keep us looking forward to that important embarkation on the family trip. It feeds the frenzy and makes the whole thing more fun.

Whenever one is planned, I always go through the same things in my head: expense, time off; can I really do this, should I really do this? In the end, the answer is always the same. Who can miss it? It's a family legacy, and I belong to the family. We cherish this tradition. I am all too aware that it has a limited life span, so in the immortal words of Sister Phyllis: "never miss a chance for an adventure!" Anywhere you go with my mother is a guaranteed adventure.

Occasionally I get the strange urge to do adjunct teaching. I love interacting with those awestruck freshmen. They crack me up, and I get a chance to try to normalize the crazy place that is college. Teaching is a refreshing change of pace. I was teaching an Introduction to Psychology at Arkansas State University a few years back. I was aware that Keith Urban had a tour date scheduled at the Convocation Center. I had not planned to go. I was lecturing in one of the big rooms with stadium seating. Mid-lecture, the door exploded open and my mother shot in. Her red hair was stuck up and out in all directions. She jumped/trotted/tripped her way down several risers and her arm shot up in the air. She yelled, "Got Keith Urban tickets, pick you up at 6!"

With that being said, she hopped up and down a couple times and ran up the risers and out of the room. Yep, always an adventure. A peak experience, definitely. The look on those students' faces, priceless. Keith Urban, a wonderful concert. Spontaneous concert run with my mom, no words can do it justice. Peak experience.

Many different things trigger peak experiences. Many people and relationships trigger peak experiences. Day to day life also produces peak experiences. A self-actualizing person is always looking for a peak experience to observe, draw in some valuable oxygen, stop, and stare gratefully. Then they wrap that experience up and store it in their heart. These experiences are gifts that God places in unexpected places at the most perfect time.

The sky is very frequently a peak experience for me. Looking up into the heavens and seeing a gorgeous blue sky with pristine white clouds placed gracefully within the blue never fails to give me pause to thank my God for the view, the smile, and the peace that permeates my soul at that moment in time. The sun, shining through the clouds with the rays appearing as lighted pathways to Heaven emit indescribable peace and admiration for what life can hand you at any given time.

Flowers, all kinds, colors, textures, and scents are a display of God's smile. Recently I noticed that my grandma's old house was being renovated. I watched it for days trying to get up the nerve to approach the workers to ask permission to see if her gardens still were alive. Then the skies opened and poured.

This, grandma had taught me, was prime flower poaching time. I drove up to the house and knocked on the door as there were a couple trucks and boots on the porch. Unfortunately, the new renter opened the door. Cautiously I explained my craziness to her. She was actually very excited as she had recently divorced and she (a fellow plant lover) had had to leave all her flowers and was not in a position to buy more. We walked the yard together, me pulling back unkempt over grown bushes and showing her the many flowers that my grandma had lovingly planted. I pulled a few more. I was also invited back to help her find the later sprouting ones and to get a few more for myself.

It was such a wonderful feeling to stroll through those gardens again. It touched my heart that something so lovingly planted and nursed still thrives after years of neglect. My heart swelled with peace. Peak experience.

Sitting outside on a beautiful afternoon, smelling honeysuckle on the breeze, reflecting on the day. Always a peak experience. Sitting on the deck of a ship with a goombay smash, watching the water, feeling the wind, smelling and gazing at the sea. Perfection.

These are just a few examples of how peak experiences awaken our senses, speak to our heart. Thus, feeding our souls and giving faith that life is good and has a purpose larger and grander that we can even begin to comprehend. They give us what we need to see the positives and build on the positives. They downplay the negatives making them appear to be miniscule, if the person is self-actualizing.

A non-self-actualizing person tends to do the opposite. They focus and dwell on every negative they see. They even are able to observe peak experiences and twist them into negative signs, events. Most often though, they do not even see or recognize these God given events. At the very least, a non-self-actualizing person cannot appropriately appreciate, if they even notice a peak experience. Why?

Peak experiences are about balance. They are about feeding the positivity, healthy knowledge and understanding of self. The base needs must be met, or at least in process of transition. Again, in moving through Maslow's hierarchy of needs, the self develops at a healthy pace, thus they are moving upward. Those growing upward are open to every positive experience or lesson. They are safe and are growing. Peak experiences are food and sustenance.

Likewise, in an unhealthy relationship, one acquired through fishing in the wrong pond, peak experiences, if present are most likely not noticed. If they are noticed, they are probably misinterpreted as nonconsequential. However, for the emotionally healthy person who is at peace with self and their own intrinsic value, the goal is different. This person has done or is doing the self-work. This person has defined what kind of relationship that will enhance their already healthy stable life. They believe and trust that with patience and with open heart and mind, they can find someone who they feel can and possibly will become the perfect luxury to bring into their life. They do not need this person; they want to share their life in a luxurious adventure.

This luxurious adventure needs peak experiences to solidify, to paint reminders in our heart that this is luxury, to make memories of small things that fill our hearts with love and joy.

Since they have been old enough to express opinions, my children have made fun of hubby and I for our bed time ritual. When I retire to bed before hubby, which is most nights, we have a long-term ritual. Hubby tucks me into bed, kisses me, tells me how much he loves me and turns off my light. It's a silly thing, I realize this, but it holds deep meaning for the both of us.

I have a friend who enjoys her bath as much as I do mine. Her husband prepares her bath for her. A small, seemingly small gesture that speaks volumes. He loves being her luxury enough that he makes this gesture to enhance a personal luxury of hers into a grand, romantic and luxurious gesture. Beautiful.

Some nights ago, my son had a class cancel. He got to spend an unexpected afternoon and night with his wife. I received a text from my daughter in law that he had flipped her off. I told her to tell him that he needed to be nice. The next text was that he was serenading her with his ukulele, singing a song that judging from the title, I am glad I do not know. I asked her if she was happy to have him home. I received an all caps YES! A peak experience.

A few years ago, a coworker and close friend of mine was at meetings at the main office all day on Valentine's Day. Her husband showed up with flowers, balloons, and a singing/dancing stuffed animal and decorated her office for her return that afternoon. They have been married longer than hubby and I have, yet he relished in this romantic act for his wife. Peak experience.

Many years ago, my whole family was at the lake. Several of us were riding in the time-challenged speed boat my parents had bought. Sister Phyllis was lounging comfortably on a seat in the front area of the boat. Hubby cut the boat at a sharp left, at which time we discovered that Phyllis' seat was not anchored to the boat. Phyllis rolled very indelicately, ass-over-tea-kettle all around the boat, coming to rest on her back with her feet and arms in the air.

My brother in law marched from the back of the boat to the front to help his beautiful wife up from her situation. Fighting back laughter he said, "these crazy women in this family, you can't live with them, but can't even imagine living without them!!!" Peak experience.

These peak experiences occur within each nuance of the world and in our lives and relationships. They are there for a reason; we need them to sustain self and belonginess to the world and to relationships. This is the reason we need to be well on the road to self-actualizing to identify a person who may become our luxury in life. We need to be able to identify the positives and mainstays of who we are. From that point, we can identify and outline what attributes constitute a luxury for the self that we are.

Once these steps are done, we are able to mingle within the world around us and value all souls we meet but recognize and gravitate toward the soul that fits the description that our soul desires as a luxury for the self that we have grown into. We also can recognize that the soul we are mingling with has the openness to grow alongside us as we continue the growth of self that never ends. The soul to walk, run, fly with us through this luxury that God has given us, the luxury of life. Enjoy every day, even the hard ones. Experience every adventure you are handed. Give thanks every day for the luxury that is life and for the luxury that you have found to share it with!

# The Collective Mother

Simple things your mother should have taught you but may not have.

1. Men are a luxury, not a necessity!
2. Never shop for a mate at court, or at court ordered events
3. No man ever died from a 'hard on' and never will, unless he took too much Viagra and is too proud to admit it.
4. Virginity is a concept, not a physical state. Rape or incest cannot 'take' virginity.
5. Virginity is a gift to be given without coercion to someone who has earned the right to be loved by you.
6. Physical love should always be an expression of emotional love and trust.
7. Do not give of your body to anyone who has not earned your trust.
8. Do not allow yourself to become anyone's property.
9. Do not neglect to teach your children. It is first and foremost your responsibility.
10. Anyone any time can break the cycle of abuse. Let it be you.
11. Every person on this earth is one of God's creatures, even if a person is someone you cannot be a mate to, they still deserve respect when you are walking away.
12. Violence is never the answer.
13. Violence should never be a secret.
14. If they are in a hurry to commit, be in a bigger hurry to run away.
15. Jealousy is uncomfortable and unnecessary; if you have a reason to be jealous, walk away: if you are jealous without cause, work on self.
16. People need people. We are all interconnected.
17. Judge not, just walk away.

18. Do not take some one home on a first date; anyone can pretend to be harmless for a couple hours.
19. Do not plan a wedding on a first date: 1. Enjoy the adventure, 2. Test the water, 3. Build trust, 4. dive in.
20. Never miss the chance for an adventure. (most valuable lesson I learned from Phyllis)
21. Always choose adventures where you have backup. "Alone" and "adventure" do not belong in the same sentence or event.
22. Friends are indispensable.
23. Do not trust anyone who wants to dispose of your friends and family.
24. Internet dating, while a fact of life these days, must not be done with abandon for safety. As a therapist, I have picked up the pieces from this one way too many times.
25. If you do not want children, do not have them. There is no return policy.
26. There are no disposable people, even the high maintenance ones with eternal Kool-Aid stains or never-ending screaming, or the ones who try to destroy themselves.
27. If you make it up out of the crap, reach back and give someone else a hand.
28. Respect your parents; anyone who buys and washes your undies deserves no less.
29. Shit happens; clean it up and move on.
30. Support, love, and depend on family. It's your right to have and your responsibility to give.
31. Someone always should know where you are and who you are with.
32. Always say I love you.
33. Stuff is irrelevant. People are not.
34. Always find something to praise.
35. You may be the prince or princess, but momma's still the Queen!
36. No one can have too many people who love them.
37. No one is perfect.
38. Do not place anyone on a pedestal; it's a long, inevitable fall!
39. Blood is not thicker than water. In fact, blood is irrelevant to the concepts of love and family

40. Never search for a new man in the acute inpatient mental health facility that you are a guest of because you overdosed over the current man or woman as the case may be.
41. Pray every day.
42. Hug someone every day.
43. Control does not equal love.
44. Start over every day.
45. Count your blessings every day.
46. Always try to have a couple bucks in the visor of your car, just in case.
47. Always have a safety net.
48. Always tell the ones you love goodnight.
49. Do something just for you at least once every day.
50. Do at least one thing for someone every day, just because.
51. Always take the opportunity to say a kind word.
52. Know who has your back.
53. Know who never has your back even when they proclaim to.
54. Kiss your luxury every day at least once and tell them how much you love them.
55. Know thyself. Know what gives you energy, know what boosts your faith, know what relaxes you, know what gives you peace, and practice each one every day.
56. Know and understand that life is change, to adapt and to overcome and turn it into an adventure is to live well.
57. Laugh every day.
58. Cry when you need to.
59. Ask for help when you need it.
60. Give help when you can.

*Marriage/Co-Habitation Contract*
Marriage/Cohabitation contract between:

_____

_____

Disagreements: State how you agree to handle disagreements, state use of fair fighting techniques to be used. Identify signal for time out. Identify how you will plan to resolve issues.

_____

_____

_____

_____

_____

_____

_____

ABSOLUTE DEAL BREAKER—violence.
Sex: Identify what you will and will not do sexually. Make a plan for how often you want to have sex.

_____

_____

_____

_____

_____

_____

_____

ABSOLUTE DEAL BREAKER—use of force or violence.
In-laws and extended family: Identify how you will handle issues with your in-laws and extended family. Make a plan for how you will handle over stepping boundary issues.

_____

_____

_____

_____

_____

_____

_____

Holidays: Identify how you will divide up holidays or if you will start your own traditions. Recognize important holiday traditions to each partner.

_____

_____

_____

_____

_____

Friends: What are the limitations you want to put on when friends come over, guys/girl's night out, times set out for just couple such as date nights and weekend date times not to be interrupted by friends?

_____

_____

_____

_____

_____

_____

DEAL BREAKER: Friend will not disrespect our spouse/significant other.
Time alone: Identify importance of time alone and how much time each will plan for alone time.

_____

_____

_____

_____

_____

_____

DEAL BREAKER- emotional isolation.
Power distribution- Identify money management plan, number of accounts, how checks will be deposited. Who will handle household expenses, limits to spending without consultation with partner, how will gifts to family members be handled and how much will they save each month? Any other power decisions and how they will be

handled, such as careers, accepting positions that require a move, hours a week set aside for work, volunteer activities.

_____

_____

_____

_____

_____

_____

_____

_____

_____

DEAL BREAKER-

Children: Identify number of children decided upon, period of time before they have children, birth control practices, and plans if accidental pregnancy occurs.

_____

_____

_____

_____

_____

_____

_____

_____

Parenting: Identify roles and expectations, will one parent stay home, if so who? What are the agreements in terms of discipline and parenting styles? Childcare arrangements, school expectations. If children are being brought into the marriage, what are the expectations of the other partner?

_____

_____

_____

_____

_____

_____

_____

_____

DEAL BREAKER: Abuse or neglect of children including emotional abuse

Religion: Identify each partner's religious preference, decisions regarding attendance, age children can decide where they attend.

_____

_____

_____

_____

_____

ABSOLUTE DEAL BREAKERS- we both agree and state what the deal breakers will be…

_____

_____

_____

_____

_____

We agree to renegotiate this contract on a regular basis of every three years and any time either spouse requests a renegotiation. At the completion of the agreed upon contract we shall share a bottle of champagne or sparkling cider by candle light in bed.

_____

Signature                                                                    Date

_____

Signature                                                                    Date

# Red Flags

There have been many sayings come and go from popularity of what each female needs in her life. I remember the, "don't go out without a dime in your shoe speech" from both Mom and Grandma. The dime was for the pay phone if you got into a situation you needed help getting out of. That was good practice and theory at that time. Things sure are different today. The list has grown considerably over time. Regarding relationships, we need to begin to understand what to look for to determine if he/she is a keeper or a throw that sucker back quick and wash your hands.

There are many signs to look for to assess for safety and for quality of relationships. There are universal red flags to help you keep safe and on track while dating and looking for Mr. or Mrs. right.

1.  If they are in a hurry, run as fast as you can in the other direction. Many abusers are in a hurry. The reason being, they are putting on an act. They are pretending to be someone they aren't. It is very hard to stay in character all the time for a long time. Thus, they are in a hurry. They proclaim love at first sight. They do not want to take things slow. If you would agree, they would move in or marry on the first date. Sorry about another fishing analogy but, they are setting the hook.

    Once the hook is set, if they slip up a little, they yank on that hook with something "special", some smoke to cover up or divert your attention from what they just did or said. There have been so many abusive marriages happen over slip ups that give a glance into reality and they hurry to divert. Marriage is a great diversion. Babies are an even greater diversion.

2.  Jealousy. If the person is irrationally jealous of everyone and even things that please you...run as fast as you can. Again,

they are trying to maintain a certain façade, and they don't want you around anyone who may be portraying the real thing, the very thing you are really looking for. They want all your time, all your energy and thoughts.

If they want to do something that does not include you…they expect you to be accountable for all your time and activities during the time they are away. They prefer strongly that you were at home alone. They will tell you this will be YOUR time, but what you can do is limited. I am not saying go out and cheat or run amok. A woman, and man, should have outside friends who are accessible within and outside of the relationship.

If you can only see your friends within your significant other's presence, you are being monitored like a child on a playground. A teacher cannot expect all children to behave and stay safe; they must be supervised. If you have done nothing to break trust, then you do not need supervision to be with friends. If you can't go with a friend to an event that your significant other would not care for, you have a problem. Most likely, abuse is either already on the scene or coming down that track at break neck speed…pardon the pun.

3. Isolation is an extension of number two but it bears teasing out on its own. Abusive people isolate their significant other. They find ways, creative ways, to end friendships, associates, work colleagues, and finally even family. If they start putting your family down and refusing to go around or refusing to allow you to go around, you are in trouble. They are building your cell. Many do not allow their significant others to work, even if they want to. Calling Mom is a no-no. Many even insist on moving away, too far for a visit with you. This cuts off your support system, and you are totally dependent on someone who only has their interest at heart, and it most likely doesn't include your safety and peace of mind.

Not only does this isolate and control you, think about children born into this situation. Children born into this situation only have two people to bond with, to watch and learn from. They are going to learn mistrust and that no one cares for them. You may take your partner's beatings or berating, but you are not teaching children belongingness. You are not giving them a sense of safety or of community. You are not, no matter how hard you try, giving them security.

4. Criticism. Nothing you say or do is right. A luxury should be your biggest fan, your best cheerleader.

Someone who wants to be necessary to you wants to be your total compass. A faulty compass at that, they will find something wrong with everything you say or do.

This serves to break you down and keep you dependent on only them. They want you to feel dependent and stupid, so they go to great lengths to shove that idea down your throat. They strip away your self-esteem.

If you were born into an unhealthy relationship, you are already groomed for this one and it is almost like there is a target on your head. They can see you a mile away. They prefer you because it's easier.

5. Addictions. Addictions are another reason to take your time and enjoy the courtship. Addictions can be hidden for a while. But once they come to light, the consequences are quite substantial.

Those who are addicted live a different kind of life style. No matter what they may say to you, what kind of promises they may make, more than likely, they see their luxury as their addiction, to which you must take at least second place.

Living with someone with an addiction is difficult, uncertain, and dangerous. You, as the significant other, are slowly dragged in. You may not become addicted yourself, but you will play a role.

Many people who have never felt belongingness, being a part of family, or needed are perfect to set up as an enabler. Before long, you are helping your significant other maintain their drug or whatever addiction they have.

You help obtain it, maintain it, hide it, and provide excuses for it. You may find yourself living in nothing like your idealization of luxury and instead in the squalor of addiction. Addiction often runs hand in hand with abuse and there you are. You have fished in the wrong pond.

Do you want to live and raise a family while splashing around in this pond? The effects last for generations, even if you eventually get out. So, don't go in. If you are already in, no matter how deep, swim for shore!

6.  Money bags. We have all seen that person that flings money around on a date or just in general like it is water from a never-ending stream. It may be fun to be spoiled like your parents may have done on your birthday or on Christmas, but even they only did it a couple times a year.

    There is a reason for that. This person throwing money and resources around is creating a smoke screen. A smoke screen keeps you from seeing the real situation. They are most likely hiding something. And at least one thing they are hiding is that there is an end to the money supply.

    Please do not misunderstand me because most all couples have financial worries at some point in time. They budget, ask for help, ask for extensions, and reduce expenditures. However, if your whole relationship is built around what he can or will buy you.... big problem. Suddenly the relationship collapses with the bank.

    In addition, if you are attracted to someone just for resources to take care of your every whim, you need some self-work. Money can't fix problems, money can't buy happiness, and money can't buy emotional security.

    Throw this one back and do some inner child work, review Maslow's Hierarchy and look at what you are missing. Work yourself through to that magical point where you are happy and healthy of self; then sling a hook in the water.

7.  Developmentally stuck. Many people are developmentally stuck somewhere along the way. They aren't looking for a luxury; they are looking for someone to either push them through or to be stuck with them. They are going to look for someone who is developmentally stuck in a similar place, so do some self-examination. If you find yourself whole and really ready for a luxury, then you've found a groupie.

    They want you to make them whole along with you. It's a nice sentiment, and these are the ones that want you to be their everything. They want a momma, a daddy, a nurse maid, and a teacher to do all the work for them on Maslow's levels. Simply said, they want you to fix them, and then you can have a great relationship.

Unfortunately, this doesn't work. You didn't take them to raise. It is very difficult to raise a spouse and children at the same time. In essence, that is what happens when you find yourself attached to someone who is emotionally stuck. Throw them back

It is important to note here that YOU could be the one who is emotionally stuck. If this is the case, go for a swim then lie on the beach and do the inner child and adult work to discover who you are and where you want to be. Once you are dry and well grounded, cast off and good luck.

8. Dysfunction. When you meet someone dysfunctional and/or from a dysfunctional family, fasten your seatbelts. It's going to be a bumpy ride. Dysfunctional families that do not exist in the state of nurturing well-grounded and rounded children, do not, in fact, raise emotionally healthy adults. In addition, they most likely have no intention of allowing their offspring to have and maintain a healthy relationship.

This one is iffy at best. It can make it, but the amount of work involved is indescribable. The heartaches, family fights, and disrespect can easily break a relationship into shards of a soul. The chosen one's family will disrupt, overbear, and overthrow every part of the couple's life.

What is worse is that the companion is probably shaky at best in emotional stability. This is a family cycle, and it is hard to break. The companion you have chosen has to choose to break that cycle, and you have no say in the matter.

If the chosen companion decides to overcome the family dysfunction, it will require much inner work, and you can only give support and what understanding you can gain.

Even if the chosen companion decides to do the work (hopefully through therapy), you still have in-laws that are dysfunctional and will continue to interfere and manipulate your companion and relationship. When children come into play, the interference heightens and the companion must stand strong and defend his new improved version of family or the family will fall quickly back into dysfunction, taking you with it. If you meet the family and see dysfunction like abuse, alcohol or drug abuse, disrespectful communication, manipulation and game playing or other dysfunctions, remember this is how the companion was raised, and this is what the companion sees as normal.

If this is something that you can live and work with the companion on meeting somewhere in the middle, then good luck, but know you are taking on moving a mountain.

If you think it's too big of a mountain to try to move, whisper a prayer of thanks for the lesson, then examine yourself for what attracted you to that dynamic and do any necessary personal inner work. When you understand, then bait your hook and cast again in a clear, calm lake.

9.  Manipulation. Manipulation is a form of dysfunction. It is used rampantly in unhealthy relationships. It is like a snake in the grass. It moves steadily and quietly before it bites. Unlike snake bites, manipulation is painless and transparent for a while.

    It starts early in a relationship with small things such as, "I really like it when someone makes a chocolate cake just for me" in such a way that you whip that cake right up while being watched from a comfy chair...don't be surprised if the cake just isn't good enough. The companion won't say it's a bad cake verbally; it will come in signals or even the famous, "it's not like my mom's." Bam, you are full out into learning to make the perfect chocolate cake. Two hours in, you're crying into your dish towel while the companion eats the cake that he proclaimed inedible. He has just taken control, and the manipulation will escalate little by little. Eventually it normally escalates to violence to ensure manipulation continues to work.

    A healthier route would be, "I sure am hungry for a chocolate cake, could we go to the store then go watch a movie or listen to music and make the cake together?" Two hours later you are snuggled together watching a movie with a chocolate cake. This scenario is a bonding experience born out of love of chocolate cake. The pattern will extend to many things the couple will learn they enjoy together. Some will even evolve into family traditions. In a few years, one night a week may be family baking night, and everyone has big desserts that they helped make, and the subsequently acquired kids are fully in on the tradition. The kitchen will look like hell, but the family will be happy, feel bonded, and know in their soul that they belong.

What seems like a simple activity can turn into a generation's long tradition that gets carried on. Imagine how you will smile seeing your child and grandchildren making and decorating cookies on baking night with the movie ready to go. Maybe instead the music will be blasting and everyone will be dancing round the table. Know the difference between an act of manipulation and an honest attempt to bond.

10. The narcissist. I intentionally did not capitalize narcissist. Only a narcissist would be offended; everyone else would assume typo.

This is your first clue. EVERYTHING is about the companion, and it always will be. Narcissism is a personality disorder, that normally very little healing, or changing takes place.

If you make a mistake, there will be no empathy or assistance from the companion. Instead expect to be berated and "punished" in some way for embarrassing them.

You are their trophy, and they will dictate everything and YOU WILL COMPLY. Your only function is to make them look better, not just better, but perfect. If you are at a function and stumble off a stiletto, the companion will catch you, pull you close and whisper biting angry words in your ear for embarrassing him. If your ankle swells up like a baseball from that bobble, he will not be empathetic. He will laugh and proclaim it your punishment from whatever Deity will make you cringe.

Please do not even let this one off the hook. Cut the line. Don't worry about the hook. It's shiny. He will consider it jewelry to distinguish himself from all the inferior fish.

# Green Lights

We have talked about "Red Lights," the thing in a relationship, a wannabe to run from, to not pass Go, do not collect $200 what dollars, but I want to share some green lights as we see them.

## How he treats his mother or the women in his life.

I'm not talking about a "momma's boy," someone who hasn't cut the apron ties, but someone who has a respect for women that hinges on their inner worth and not on how they look to the eye. This man sustains important relationships with important women in his life, maybe his Sunday school teacher or the woman who finally got him to understand fractions. He may be a natural flirt who hugs all the women he knows in Wal-Mart. He respects his mother, he visits his mother, and he honors her in her elderly years.

## He takes responsibility for his children.

He pays his child support, doesn't complain about it in front of the kids, and takes every opportunity to spend time with them yet is flexible with their schedules and wants. Children do not ask to be born; they aren't the reason your first marriage failed. If you are seriously considering getting involved in a relationship, you have to understand that this potential has a prior commitment that is called his kids. Individuals who recognize this encourage and support their partner to maintain a relationship with their kids, encourage visits, are willing to step into the role of co-parent, and don't count child support money as household income, stand a greater chance of making things work on their journey. Resenting a child because she would rather go to her grandmother on your weekend may prick your ego, but honoring your children and their desire gives an insight into your character,

## You share like morals and values.

Little and big, you discover that you have similar morals and values. He wouldn't dream of taking two papers when he put money for one in the paper box or short a waitress of a tip. He doesn't try to buy people with gifts or get something free that he doesn't deserve. The kind of stuff you may notice early on in a relationship but don't think are a big deal are a bigger deal than you think. Pay attention.

## He shares respect.

The potential luxury shows their respect of others. They recognize the worth of all people they come in contact with and those that others don't. He treats the person who over charged him with the same respect he does the umpire at the ball game. He shakes the preacher's hand and tells him or her that they did a good job; he doesn't roast the preacher at the Sunday meal after church. They don't complain about the teacher, the waiter, their boss, the banker, your mother. That doesn't mean that he and you don't discuss especially difficult encounters, because you do, but it isn't constant griping about things you and he have no control over.

All of us have hurts, sorrows, and often time horrendous events that have caused us pain. Your future luxury has learned how to let go of those hurts as much as possible. Will they be totally healed? Most likely not, but they have learned the healing art of forgiveness. They have let go of the pain associated with the event. They no longer recount every horrible thing that has ever happened to them when the next horrible thing happens. If they have been cheated on and lied to by a previous spouse, they have let go of that hurt and don't drag it into their new relationship.

## Knows how to process and sets goals.

Your companion on this journey understands and accepts that life and love are a process and is willing to do the hard work to get there. Relationships that end because "they don't love their partner anymore" often are ones in which the partners didn't know how or are unwilling to do the hard work of staying together. They have expected life to stay in the lust; her world revolves around me stage. They haven't grown through the events of life nor have they learned to support their luxury. Often, they haven't learned to move on with their partner. They haven't set relationship goals and have just let life batter them against rocky shores, over and over. They haven't sought a way beyond the trauma; a luxury walks the walk with you. They support you through the traumas of life just as you support them, and when you get to the other side of the trauma the relationship has grown.

## Has a sense of humor and can laugh at himself.

Life sometimes just sucks, and you have to find a way to laugh at things. A luxury can laugh at themselves at the times where crying seems what others would do, just as Nena's luxury fell out of a boat onto dry land and broke his arm and elbow, my luxury has done some real dingers. He had two fingers torn off when his hand caught in a machine at work. In the emergency room, he looked his doctor in the eye while his doctor was scrubbing his mangled and numb hand and told him, "That looks like it should hurt." Or when he laughs because he can't hold change in his left "because it falls through his hand." Or my luxury's humor of the Sherriff's office calling in the middle of the night and picking up the phone without answering it, hands me the receiver, and says, "It's for you. Who else gets phone calls in the middle of the night?"

## They know how to have fun.

Everyone needs down time, needs time to recuperate from the pressures of work, from raising a family and, yes, even from being a partner. Our luxuries know how to have fun, most times with us but sometimes without. We have been on vacations with and without our spouses, with and without our families. Your hobbies don't have to be the same as your significant other, and in fact, if we did everything together life might be boring. We have always taken time out to have fun. We have camped in tents with small children; we have gone on cruise ships with teenagers and have been to a mountain cabin with just another couple. We have stayed in the budget motels or camped on the beach. No matter where you go or what you do, fun strengthens relationships. It gives you time to breathe and make memories so that when life is hard, when we are bombarded by the hard stuff, we can draw on the fun times to get us through.

## Self-Assessment

| Basic Needs and Shelter | Circle (T) or (F) to answer True or False to following questions following questions |
|---|---|
| T        F | I am able to feed myself and my family without getting food assistance, |
| T        F | My utilities have been on all year. |
| T        F | I live alone or have a roommate arrangement. |
| T        F | I have been homeless in the last year. |
| T        F | I have access to transportation |
| T        F | I am able to get health care as needed |
| T        F | I have been evicted in the last 3 years, |
| T        F | I do my own laundry. |
| T        F | I am able to cook a well-balanced meal. |
| T        F | I bathe or shower at least 3x's a week. |
| T        F | I brush my hair and teeth daily. |
| **Interpersonal Skills** | Circle (T) or (F) to answer True or False to following questions following questions. |
| T        F | I am estranged from one or more of my family members. |
| T        F | I have been fired or let go from a job for not getting along with coworkers and/or supervisors. |
| T        F | I have a difficult time controlling my temper or have been called hot headed. |
| T        F | I am able to maintain friendships over time. |
| T        F | I would rather be alone than with people. |
| T        F | I think most people can't be trusted. |

| T | F | I can communicate my thoughts and feelings with respect. |
|---|---|---|
| T | F | I work to have a drama free life. |
| T | F | I am capable of recognizing and meeting the needs of others. |
| **Self Esteem** | | Circle (T) or (F) to answer True or False to following questions following questions |
| T | F | I like what I see in the mirror. |
| T | F | I am a valuable part of my family and my community. |
| T | F | I think I have grown as a person. |
| T | F | I make an effort to work on me. |
| T | F | I have a purpose in life. |
| T | F | Without a partner in life I feel incomplete, |
| **Employment and career** | | Circle (T) or (F) to answer True or False to following questions following questions. |
| T | F | I have completed high school. |
| T | F | I have completed either a training program or higher education degree |
| T | F | I am currently employed in my chosen field. |
| T | F | I have been fired from more than one job. |
| T | F | I am disabled and draw disability. |
| T | F | I am unemployed and have been unemployed for more than 6 months. |
| T | F | I dropped out of high school. |
| T | F | I have or am serving in the military. |
| T | F | I was dishonorably discharged from service. |
| T | F | I have been recognized as a model employee. |
| T | F | I am able and willing to follow instructions. |
| T | F | I only miss work for legitimate illness or family emergency. |
| **Sexuality** | | Circle (T) or (F) to answer True or False to following questions following questions. |
| T | F | I am comfortable with discussing sex with a partner. |

| | | |
|---|---|---|
| T | F | I use masturbation to relieve tension and to give myself pleasure. |
| T | F | I am sexually active. |
| T | F | I take responsibility for birth control. |
| T | F | I get pleasure when I am in control and inflict pain. |
| T | F | I want to be submissive in a relationship. |
| T | F | I expect to have sex daily. |
| T | F | I like to experience different kinds of sex including oral and anal sex. |
| T | F | I have had multiple sexual partners. |
| T | F | Sex is extremely important to me. |
| T | F | I am on the sexual perpetrators registry. |
| T | F | I was sexually abused as a child. |
| T | F | I have been a victim of rape. |
| T | F | I have never had sex. |
| T | F | The idea of having sex frightens me. |
| T | F | I have and use a safe word. |
| T | F | I am always respectful of my partner's feelings and needs. |
| T | F | Even in marriage, no means no. |
| **Family of Origin** | | Circle (T) or (F) to answer True or False to following questions following questions. |
| T | F | I had a good childhood. |
| T | F | I visit frequently with my parents and/or siblings. |
| T | F | I spend holidays with my extended family. |
| T | F | I have been in foster care as a child. |
| T | F | I am an adopted child. |
| T | F | I consult my parents before making major decisions or purchases. |
| T | F | My parents make plans and expect me to participate. |
| T | F | My parents want me to attend their church. |
| T | F | There is a history of mental illness in my family. Some of my family is "a shit pile of crazy." |

| | | |
|---|---|---|
| T | F | I am a child of divorce. |
| T | F | I grew up in a blended family and loved it. |
| T | F | I grew up in a blended family and hated it. |
| **Faith and Religion** | | Circle (T) or (F) to answer True or False to following questions following questions |
| T | F | I have a strong faith in God. |
| T | F | I'm not sure there is a God |
| T | F | I actively participate in my denomination. Write in name of your denomination:_____ |
| T | F | I am willing to attend my partner's church at times. |
| T | F | I think a family should participate in church frequently. |
| T | F | I think children should decide for themselves if they want to attend church. |
| T | F | I think you can have a strong faith and not attend church. |
| T | F | I would go to church alone if my partner refused to attend with me. |
| T | F | Faith is more than what church you attend, |
| | | |
| **Marriage** | | Circle (T) or (F) to answer True or False to following questions following questions. |
| T | F | Marriage should not be entered into lightly. |
| T | F | Marriage is just a piece of paper. |
| T | F | Marriage is for keeps, |
| T | F | Marriage is a promise to each other under God. |
| T | F | It's okay to hit your spouse. |
| T | F | It's okay to live together outside of marriage. |
| T | F | I've been married before. |
| T | F | Marriage is a way to trap someone into staying with you. |
| T | F | My examples of marriage have not been very good |
| T | F | I expect to get married at some time in the future. |

| | | |
|---|---|---|
| T | F | My examples of marriage have been good. |
| T | F | I don't know any marriage that has lasted. |
| **Children** | | Circle (T) or (F) to answer True or False to following questions following questions. |
| T | F | I have children. |
| T | F | I have custody of my children. |
| T | F | I want to have children someday. |
| T | F | My children's other parent provides financial support. |
| T | F | I would treat my partner's children as my own. |
| T | F | I would let my partner discipline my children. |
| T | F | I want to have children with my partner. |
| T | F | I use spanking for discipline. |
| T | F | I will use my parents' example when parenting my own or my partner's children. |

# What My Assessment Tells Me

## Basic Needs

If you are having a difficult time meeting your own basic needs, now is not the time to enter into a for keeps relationship. Get a job, go to school, or apply for disability. Avail yourself of community resources and programs. Join the library, get into rehab, or get some counseling. The better you can meet your own needs, the more whole of a person you become.

## Interpersonal Skills

If you have problems getting along with others, now is not the time to enter into a long-term relationship. Don't expect others to accommodate your nasty temper or your mean words. Now is the time to work on you and to find ways of developing better interpersonal skills. As therapists, Nena and I will tell you that poor interpersonal skills are often embedded in personality and take a lot of work to improve, but it isn't impossible. Find a therapist who uses cognitive behavioral therapy and really work the program. Join a support group or participate in a program like Celebrate Recovery. Volunteer somewhere you can practice the skills you gain, keep a journal of your progress and relationships. Analyze your social media interactions and see how healthy they are.

## Self-Esteem

Good self-esteem is at the very core of wholeness and, all of us suffer from issues of low self-esteem at any given time in our life. The wonderful thing about self-esteem is that just as negative events in our life effect how we feel about ourselves positive events contribute to a positive sense of self. In order to improve how we feel about ourselves, we need to find ways of developing positive events not waiting for them to just happen. Volunteer with children, the elderly, or the environment. Make friends with the neighbors who have nobody else. Take a class; join a support group or participate in therapy. Focus on what makes you feel better about yourself. There are thousands of self-help books out there. Use some of them. As a minister (Vonda), I would also recommend finding a church where you feel loved and supported, where you recognize that you are a creation of God, and God doesn't create junk. Identify one thing about yourself that you want to change and then work on that change: stopping smoking, losing weight, getting a degree help to contribute to positive self-regard; the foundation of self- esteem.

## Employment and career

We would recommend that everyone seek out some form of higher education or enrichment programing throughout their life time as a way toward wholeness. Not everyone is cut out for or interested in college. Our husbands weren't, but both have, over the years, participated in classes and programs that improved that capacity to support them and our families. Sometimes we feel stuck in a job and are dependent on the income to support their family. That doesn't mean we have to stay stuck. It isn't easy, but both Nena and I worked full time difficult jobs and went back to school to get first our BAs and then our Masters degrees because we had the support of our husbands behind us. If you can't go back to school, develop a hobby, take a painting class, become a Girl Scout or Boy Scout leader. Do something that sparks your interest, who knows? It might become a career.

## Sexuality

Sexuality is an important part of our self-identify and what we have to offer a partner in a relationship. Self-reflection is essential in discovering our own sexual attractions, needs, and desires. Society has become significantly more open on the outside when it comes to talking about sexual orientation such as straight, gay, bi-sexual, but underneath, there is often confusion, guilt, or promiscuity that keeps an individual from sexual health. If you cannot be honest with yourself, you have little, if any, chance of being honest with a partner. Histories of child sexual abuse or previous rape can have a significant impact on how an individual feel about intimacy. Unresolved issues surrounding sexual abuse or rape can impact a relationship. As therapists, we certainly recommend that individuals who have unresolved issues seek therapy or other means of self-help programs or groups to resolve these issues before entering into a long-term relationship. Being honest with a perspective partner can open up significant communication opportunities. In addition to being open regarding your history of sexual abuse, it's important to be honest about likes and dislikes sexually, sexual experience or inexperience. If we aren't honest in a relationship about what we like and don't like sexually, what turns us on and off, we cannot expect our partner to be a mind reader. Ultimately, without honesty, we risk having a sexual life that is unfulfilling or possibly one that is frightening.

## Family of Origin

Each of us have unique families of origins. Some of us have families that were nurturing, loving members who treated us with love and respect and helped us to gain the skills needed to becoming functioning adults. Others of us have families who were either physically or emotionally absent, some who were physically, emotionally, and/or sexually abusive. Our families shape us, help us to develop into functioning or nonfunctioning adults and influence how we deal with issues and problems we face as adults. In addition, our families of origin can provide ongoing support and encouragement throughout our lives. Not all families are loving and nurturing, and as adults, we have to find ways of making up for what we didn't receive from our families. There are many options and ways of helping to heal the hole left in our development by dysfunctional or absent families. Among those options are individual and group therapy, twelve-step faith-based programs like Celebrate Recovery, developing relationships with functional families who will mentor and nurture you, and involvement of with a nurturing church who help you to heal your bruised and broken places in your soul.

We cannot change our families of origin, but we can change the way we respond to the narrative that we were given. Nena and I (Vonda) had very different family of origin experiences, although we both had grandmothers who had a significant influence in our lives. I have made a point of developing supportive, loving relationships with other women both in my church and in my professional career. I think it is important to recognize that some of us were dealt a crappy hand when it came to our family of origin, but it is possible to overcome much of what we were given. As adults, we have the opportunity and responsibility to work to get past what damage we have received from our family of origins, and we need to do that before we enter into our own relationships and have children.

## Faith and Religion

Before you enter into a permanent relationship it is important that you talk about faith and religion and what your expectations are for your future family. There needs to be an understanding about how we look at faith and religion and our expectations regarding church attendance. I'm not saying that relationships that have different expectations regarding church denominations, attendance, and beliefs can't work because I have seen many that have, but they were relationships where there had been open communication about beliefs, expectations and where there was willingness to compromise.

## Marriage

Beliefs and expectations regarding marriage vary between individuals, and it is important that each of us who want to enter into a "for keeps" relationship are aware of what our expectations are regarding marriage and what that prospective partner's expectations are. If your expectations are that marriage is 'til death do you part, engaging in relationship with someone who has been married three times may be setting yourself up for heartache. Too often individuals jump into marriage with little preparation. They may have jumped into a sexual relationship and the sex is good, so they think it is time to get married. They may have already gotten pregnant and thought, "We have to be married." Those reasons are not healthy ones when that prospective partner is not a good match and not a luxury. We recommend that each prospective marital couple avail themselves of premarital therapy whenever available. Premarital therapy should help a couple identify prospect "hot spots" in their relationship, help to develop good communication skills, and will help the couple develop problem solving skills. In addition to premarital therapy, it is important that a couple who has made the commitment of marriage be willing to participate in martial therapy should issues or crisis in their lives cause problems in their marriage. Too often couples give up on their relationships when things get difficult instead of seeking marital therapy. Often this happens in relationships where there is limited communication and unwillingness to compromise.

## Children

Do you want them? Does he or she want them? Do you have them? Does he or she have them? What are your beliefs and expectations in regard to parenting, to discipline? Will your family be a blended family, and what are your expectations regarding discipline or willingness to work with step-children and their other parent? We tend to parent the way we were parented unless we make a conscious effort to do something different. Couples who have had significantly different experiences growing up and being parented may have a difficult time finding compromises. Recognizing that each child is an individual and that parenting is the most important, unending job that we can ever hold allows a couple to determine what the best way to parent their children. If you don't like children and don't want to be a parent, don't enter into a relationship with someone who has children or someone who wants them. If you agree to never to have children, discuss what you are going to do if one mysteriously appear. Accidents happen!

## When Running Away Isn't an Option

Don't get me wrong. Taking a time out away from your mate and family (a little business time, a weekend with the cousins, a church women's retreat, Summer Camp with the National Guard) can be, and often is, a necessary part of life and in fact can be very nourishing to a relationship. Nena has been known to take the occasional all girls cruise with her mother, sisters, and daughter. I, on the other hand, have went off to the woods and stayed in a cabin in the middle of winter with no running water, by choice, more than one time. But sometimes those options aren't available. There may be financial, health, work, and family commitments that just don't allow you to leave. Sometimes you are so blindsided by grief and loss that you can barely crawl out of bed that, as much as you might want to run away, the space between you and the door might as well be the Grand Canyon. You may be up to your elbows in baby vomit, two kids at home sick with the stomach bug, and you can't remember when you had your last period.

This chapter is about taking care of yourself so you can take care of what life throws you. As the old Southern saying going, "When you're up to your ass in Alligators, now is not the time to figure out how to drain the swamp." A good portion of knowing what to do when you need to escape is preplanning and preparation.

- Meditation
- Relaxation
- Diet
- Exercise
- Hobbies
- Prayer
- Friendships
- Knowing Resources
- Massage
- Creativity
- Flexibility
- Therapy
- Developing New Habits
- Social Connections
- Volunteer

## Meditation

There are lots of meditation programs out there, everything from one on one direction, CD's, computer programs, and classes. Meditation for our purposes boils down to taking time and space to put aside all that life is dealing you so that you can focus on your inner self. It is a way of remaining calm in the storm, a way to connect to your creator, the universe, your presence outside of time and space.

## Relaxation

One of the simplest ways to relax is to use a computer/cd called *Guided Imagery*. It directs you to find a safe, peaceful place and then has a sequence of steps that you see in your mind's eye. Another is the sequenced process of tightening each individual muscle group us starting with your toes, tightening and then relaxing the muscles until you have relaxed your entire body.

## Diet

During the middle of a crisis or when you are overwhelmed with life is not the time to start a diet, but now when life is on an even keel (and I hope it is), it is time to think about healthy eating. Look up the food pyramid online and see how close you fall into the daily recommended amounts in each category and if you are off, and most of us are, begin the journey to wellness by adding the stuff that is recommended and taking away some of what you eat in excess. You may not think it is a big deal, or that adding one more vegetable a day is not going to make a difference, but every little bit helps. If your body is stronger, you are less susceptible to every bug that comes along, and some of those bugs can be deadly.

## Exercise

No matter what it is, some exercise is better than no exercise. If you have to set in your wheelchair and move your feet and arms, that is better than nothing. Get a cart and walk around Walmart. Walk through your neighborhood. Say hi to the neighbors. Anything you do is going to make you feel better. Anything you do repeatedly over an extended period of time becomes a habit. Exercise releases vital chemicals in your brain that increase your sense of wellbeing.

## Hobbies

Hobbies can literally save your sanity. They can be as time consuming and intricate as stain glass work or intricate bead work. It can be as enriching to your body as gardening or as sedentary and enriching to your mind as reading. Hobbies allow you to escape while still being there. They take you away from life's daily struggles and for a period of time they allow you to only focus on that activity. Hobbies can turn into jobs, volunteer work, or a skill passed down to the next generation.

## Prayer

Whether you are religious or think there might be something out there, prayer can be a skill that can help you "walk through the shadow of the valley of death." Prayer can lighten your mood. It can help you to recognize that you are not alone. Whether it is the repetitiveness of prayers such as the Rosary, the prayers of many Eastern faith traditions, or a "Good Morning God" conversation, it is the action that counts. Prayers don't have to always be when the alligators are in the swamp. They can be of thanksgiving and praise, of drawing apart awhile to communion with God, and they can add a foundational tool that you can always count on.

## Friendships

Friendships are more than superficial acquaintances. Friendships connect us to others, they see us through the most difficult times of our lives, and they celebrate the most joyous times of our lives as well. Friendship is a wonderful and funny thing; it can happen because you went to school together, worked together, participated in a community organization together, met online, or are neighbors. The common core of friendship is that they take some effort on each of our parts. Friendships can be life lasting; the girls you hung out with in high school who come to set with you on your death bed. Or they can be intense for a period of time where you grow apart because someone moves jobs, changes, or if life just simply goes on.

## Knowing Resources

Learn the resources in your community. There are support groups, educational resources, and twelve step programs in almost every community. Some resources are even home based (they come to you). If you name an issue or a problem, I can find you some kind of support within an hour because that is what I did for years, find or develop resources. Everybody can acquaint themselves with what is available in their community. You might not need these resources now, but it pays to keep some information on what is offered in the community.

## Massage

For many people, the idea of accepting strangers' hands on their bodies in terrifying. For the rest of us, it is an experience that we can hardly wait for. Massage improves our sense of wellbeing. It allows us to relax, and it helps us to not only release our physical pain but to give up our emotional pain as well. Consider it on your list for of taking care of yourself.

## Creativity

Some of you may say you don't have a creative gene but just like Data the android on *Star Trek: The Next Generation* who strives to play the violin, all of us can kindle creativity. Whether it is writing poetry or short stories, it doesn't have to suit anyone but you. From drawing tattoo art to making concrete look like wood flooring, there are all kinds of ways to create. I learned to make really big hair bows for a granddaughter most recently, and over the last several months, crocheted a baby blanket. These things are not exactly my hobbies but are creative things I did for a special purpose. Search for a creative outlet for yourself; you'll be amazed on how it makes you feel.

## Flexibility

You may not think learning to practice flexibility is something that you need, or even something that you can practice, but it really is. Think about your life, your routine, your schedule. Now imagine that at the last minute you were told what you expected to do at 3:00 p.m. you had to do at 7:00 a.m. How does that make you feel? Does anxiety crawl up your back bone and reach around and grab you by the throat? If so, the whole idea of being flexible might be hard for you do deal with but come now let's try. Pick one thing that you insist has to be done a certain way or at a certain time. And don't do it that way. Let the dishes wait until morning or drive to work a different way. The ability to be flexible, to think on your feet when life starts throwing boulders in your part allows you the flexibility to deal.

## Therapy

We don't just recommend therapy because we are therapists, which would be like your friend the surgeon recommending you get your appendix out without examining you. We recommend therapy because we see the significant difference it can make in people's lives if they are willing to do the hard work and make the changes needed in their life to give them a greater purpose, to ease their pain and to bring about positive change. Therapists are only as good as their client and their willingness to change. Therapists can provide with you with the safety and structure to make changes. They can provide you with unconditional positive regard and compassion. They can help you identify some choices you keep making, but ultimately, that can only provide direction. You have to take the wheel.

## Developing New Habits

Developing new habits first requires that we assess the old habits we would like to break and the new habits we would like to acquire. It is always easier to acquire a new habit than to break an old one, but I have this tricky therapist thing called reframing that ANYBODY can learn to do. It means instead of saying "I want to quit smoking," you say, "I want to be a non-smoker." So instead of everyday lamenting what you are trying to stop, focus on the things you start. You say non-smokers don't smoke in their cars, therefore, I will not smoke in my car. I know you may be saying that is just semantics, but semantics can be some powerful when you use them for your greater good.

## Social Connections

Social connections are those things that make us part of the great society around us; they are something besides our relatives. Social connections can be our child's school or our work. It is where we give and take feedback about ourselves and our place in the world. It is where we take our cues no matter if they are misread about ourselves. Social connections are essential to our self-esteem and our sense of accomplishment. If you find out you have no one but your family to give you positive reinforcement on a job, increasing your social connections can help. Seeking out a church, a civic organization, a bingo game and beginning to develop some social connections will help. In every little town in the south, there is either a dance or a wrestling match. You just might find someone to talk to there. Another option is Social Media where you can connect with friends and family from across the world. I have received some tremendous support from many of my Facebook friends, but it doesn't replace being able to look someone in the eye, hear the inflection in their voice, and get the occasional hug.

## Volunteer

One of the easiest ways of not getting all sucked up into yourself and the worries that don't allow you to run away, even for a little while, is to volunteer. Volunteer at your children's school, the senior center, the town library, drive for meals on wheels, or clean out pens at the animal shelter. You can become a Girl Scout leader, a Boy Scout Leader, a 4-H leader, volunteer at the County Extension office, or become a Pink Lady at the hospital. Think about giving back to your community, your church, or the neighborhood. Volunteers are needed in every community in the country.

Too often we find people that just give up. They sit looking at four walls in miserable relationships, in sadness, overwhelmed by life and the hand they have been dealt. They may now be empty nesters; maybe they are even single again due to death or divorce. Maybe they are no longer able to do a job that they loved due to illness or disability. They have given up. The glass doesn't have to be either half full or half empty. Grab another smaller glass and let it be overflowing. Our lives do not have to stagnate; they can be full with abundance, but we have to be willing to take care of ourselves. We have to be willing to acknowledge that, "We are a luxury."

# Belonging Verses Being Trapped

We would do you, the reader, a disservice if this book about becoming your best self and finding your luxury in life didn't address the difficulties that long-term relationships sometimes have. The erectile dysfunction commercials have a distinguished looking gentleman usually with a younger looking woman finding sexual fulfillment with a little pill and falling in love all over again. Face it. Sex sells, and society would look aghast if the rotund gentleman was trying to get his wife from her walker into the matching bath tubs so they could hold hands in sexual fulfillment or if the commercials showed a couple who had been through life's ups and downs and, although they still had all their parts, had learned that intimacy and completeness could happen and does happen to many couples without the need to still "do it like bunnies." Often there are times in each couple's relationship where toys and aids might bring back some spark if you think that is missing or the couple may just want a beach in Cozumel looking out on the ocean to bring a sense of joy and fulfillment.

Sometimes one or both partners in a long-term relationship have a sense of panic, a time of questions about, "Is this all there is out there?" Marriages of forty years break up because someone feels trapped or catches the eye of someone on the outside of the relationship, most likely in their work environment, and the promises and commitments made in their marriage don't seem to be that big of a deterrent to straying as maybe they were in the past. All of us know couples who everyone thought always would be together who suddenly aren't, and like the ripple effect of a stone thrown in the pond, the people around them begin to question their own life and choices. Life at this stage can either become a stage of belonging and acceptance or one uprooted with regrets and feels of being trapped.

One of the greatest hurdles to cross when these feelings come into a marriage or a long-term relationship is to recognize that each party has a right to "feel" the way he or she does because feelings are emotions that we just have. It is when we turn those feelings into action that we can either enrich or destroy the relationship. Communication with your partner now is just as important as it was in the early days of the relationship. Telling your partner that you feel taken for granted or that you lack sexual satisfaction isn't saying you want out of the marriage or this relationship. It is opening yourself up to identifying things that can be done together, so that, in turn, the way you feel about things might change. Communication allows us to make a paradigm shift, to see things from the other's perspective. When we can look at life from a different perspective, how we feel about things in our lives can change, and sometimes you need to hang on tight because the changes that can happen might just knock your socks off. It may be as simple as "After all these years I'm going to start dressing up a little because I like the reaction I get from you when I do," to as life changing as, "I'm going to file for my disability, make candles in my spare time, and join you on the book tour."

You see, belonging together doesn't mean that you have to feel trapped in the old same old, same old. It can be as freeing as we are going to take the travel trailer and see as much of our world as we can together or as bonding as we are going to take up a new hobby together so that we can strengthen our ties and interests. It may be having a couples' massage and getting that hot tub you always said you would like or at least going to the spa and pretending that the hot tub belongs to you alone.

Our bodies change, and we can't do all the things we used to, but that doesn't mean that our commitment, our bonding, or even our love affair with each other has to change. It does mean that we may need to think outside our familiar box as to what constitutes intimacy for us. We live in an age where the chances are that our life span may be greater than our parents and where marital aids, (the euphoniums for sex toys) are available from parties you host in your own home to the shelf at Wal-Mart next to the lubricants and condoms. If climax is what you need or are looking for, most can achieve it, but it may take a little work. Intimacy at any stage of life doesn't require sex in and of itself. Intimacy can be the morning or evening cuddle, snuggling up on the porch in a blanket, and watch the rain run off the roof. It may be holding hands in church, at the movies, or the occasional kiss just to get a reaction from the grandkids. It's saying "I love you" at the end of every phone call or the end of a long day or just before you walk out of the house. Intimacy knows you belong; as long as you are willing to expand your relationship, keep having fun within your limitations no matter what they may be, and put in the effort required you will not be trapped, you will not be trapped. You will belong.

# Our Summary

We believe life's journey should be about getting from birth to the grave as whole, as self-actualized as we can become, and in that process, if we should desire we can join with a partner, a companion, a luxury to share that adventure. We all start our adventure as part of someone else's journey and, through life events, slowly the adventure becomes our own journey. At some point as stated above, most people begin to desire belongingness and start shopping for a mate, hopefully one who will be your lasting luxury.

We have written this book with self-revelation and humor in hopes that not only our professional colleagues, but our families, friends, and the general public might find some direction for the journey worthy of consideration. We wish you much laughter, many adventures, and constant love. Enjoy! And please let us know what you think at lifebeyondtheory@gmail.com

# References

Ames, Richard F. "Five Keys to a Successful Marriage," July-August 2007. www.tomorrowworld.org.

Bloom, Linda LCSW and Charlie Bloom, MSW: "7 Steps to Healing Broken Trust," www.huffingtonpost.com.

Briggs, David. "5 Ways Faith Contributes to Strong Marriages, New Studies Suggest," *The Blog, Huffingtonpost.com*

*www.goodtherapy.org/blog/psychpedia/maslov-hierarchy-needs*

Center of Marriage and Family at Creighton University (1999)

National Health Statistics Report, 2012

Nortare, Theresa and H. Richard McCord, "Marriage and the Family in the United States, Resources for Society." (2001). *United States Conference of Catholic Bishops*

"Why Marriage Matter; Thirty Conclusions from the Social Sciences, The Institute for American Values and the National Marriage Project." (2011).

Wilcox, Bradford W., "The State of our Unions: Marriage in America" 2011 (University of Virginia Nat*ional Marriage Project*, Charlottesville, VA)

CPSIA information can be obtained
at www.ICGtesting.com
Printed in the USA
BVHW03s2206240618
519874BV00027B/219/P

9 781982 204143